business *masterminds*

# peter
# DRUCKER

## ROBERT HELLER

A Dorling Kindersley Book

www.dk.com

## Dorling Kindersley

LONDON, NEW YORK, AUCKLAND, DELHI, JOHANNESBURG,
MUNICH, PARIS, SYDNEY and TORONTO

DK www.dk.com

Senior Editor Adèle Hayward
Senior Art Editor Caroline Marklew
Project Art Editors Christine Lacey,
Laura Watson
DTP Designer Jason Little
Production Controller Elizabeth Cherry

Managing Editor Stephanie Jackson
Managing Art Editor Nigel Duffield

Produced for Dorling Kindersley by
Grant Laing Partnership 48 Brockwell
Park Gardens, London SE24 9BJ
Senior Editor Jane Laing
Project Editor Helen Ridge
Managing Art Editor Steve Wilson

**Author's Acknowledgments**
The many sources for this book have been
acknowledged in the text, but I must now
express my great debt to everybody, above
all to the Mastermind himself. Nor would
the book exist but for the inspiration and
effort of the excellent Dorling Kindersley
team – to whom my warm thanks.

**Packager's Acknowledgments**
Grant Laing Partnership would like to
thank the following for their help and
participation:
Editorial Lee Stacy, Frank Ritter;
Design Sarah Williams;
Index Kay Ollerenshaw.

**Publisher's Acknowledgments**
Dorling Kindersley would like to thank the
following for their help and participation:
Editorial Josephine Bryan, Claire Ellerton,
Nicola Munro, Jane Simmonds;
Design Austin Barlow, Tracy Hambleton-
Miles, Nigel Morris;
DTP Rob Campbell, Louise Waller;
Picture research Andy Sansom.

**Picture Credits**
The publisher would like to thank the
following for their kind permission to
reproduce the following photographs:
**Corbis UK Ltd:** Bettmenn 9; **General
Motors Corporation:** GM Media Archives
12, 20; **Robert Harding Picture Library:**
Nigel Francis 38, Andrew Mills 59; **Hulton
Getty:** 17, 72; **Image Bank:** Archive Photos
79; **Tony Stone Images:** Frank Cezuz 95 53,
Mary Kate Denny 88, Walter Hodges 34,
Kaluzny/Thatcher 53; **Telegraph Colour
Library:** Harry Bartlett 62, Robin Davis 50,
G Germany 28; **Times Syndication:** 2.

Front jacket: **Times Syndication.**

# Contents

# The management pioneer

**M**ore than any other thinker, Peter Drucker created the concept of management as an intellectual and practical discipline. He has bridged at least four worlds: academic teaching, journalism, consultancy, and socio-economic history. Drucker's wealth of experience has produced a unique blend of intellectual rigour, popularization, practicality, and deep understanding of crucial trends. Most of the economic and management ideas that influence theorists and practising managers today trace back to, and are still inspired by, Drucker's work.

They include the main methods used to make the divided organization and managers more effective − notably the principle and practice of Management by Objectives. His work on managing and achieving innovation is itself an example of innovative thought, which has become crucial in the "knowledge society" that Drucker was first (in 1969) to identify and describe. His greatest strength is his ability to interpret the present − to see, before anybody else, what is actually happening in society, the economy, and corporations. In consequence, his management observations often go against the crowd, but into the heart of the matter.

*Robert Heller*

# Biography

Peter Drucker was born in 1909 in Vienna. Even though he has lived in America for over 60 years, the influences and memories of middle Europe in general, and Vienna in particular, are still strong. Despite his heavy German accent, Drucker is an English speaker of astonishing clarity and fluency, whose logic is remorseless, and who has seemingly perfect recall of the facts, figures, and anecdotes that he uses in profusion to illustrate his ideas.

His writings have been more widely read, and have embodied more breakthroughs, than those of any other management thinker. But it is Drucker's appearances as a teacher, both in universities and in all manner of management forums, that have indelibly impressed two generations of practising managers. He represents in the US today the mid-European intellectual tradition into which he was born, combining academic distinction with practical application.

## Multi-disciplined intellectual

Drucker's lawyer father was the top civil servant in the Ministry of Economics in the Austro-Hungarian Empire. His mother, unusually for the time, had been a medical student. His intellectal family (they knew Freud and many other Viennese luminaries) were in very comfortable circumstances. Living in such a cultured family played a major part in Drucker's education. The cultured ease, however, was harshly interrupted by the horrors of World War I, which broke out when Drucker was five: its end brought near-famine to Austria.

After finishing his schooling at the Gymnasium in Vienna, Drucker left for a clerk's desk in a Hamburg exporting company. To please his parents, he studied law in Hamburg: he also read voluminously in three languages and published his first article. Then he moved to Frankfurt to work for a Wall Street firm as a trainee analyst, carrying on with his law studies, and studying statistics as well. His familiarity and ease with numerical facts and their meaning has been a major factor in his accurate, often uncannily prescient, reading of today and tomorrow.

His interest in current events, and in numbers, makes it seem natural that he became a financial journalist after the collapse of his employer in the Wall Street crash of 1929. He won rapid promotion on Frankfurt's largest paper, and also got a doctorate at the university, where he met Doris Schmitz, a successful technologist, who would later become his wife. While Drucker worked as a newspaper correspondent abroad, German society was disintegrating: the triumph of Fascism was the spur for his first book, *The End of Economic Man: The Origins of Totalitarianism* (1939). Not surprisingly, it was published after 1933, when Drucker left Hitler's Germany for good.

# Humanitarian thinker

The book, a hostile examination of the deep irrationality of Fascism, established one of the main strands in Drucker's philosophy. He is a humanitarian thinker, who approaches business, management, and economics as aspects of social and political history, not as ends in themselves. His profound understanding of 20th-century tides has conditioned his management thought. So has his experience of practical matters, including a spell in London, where he

**General Motors in wartime**
*Alfred P. Sloan (left) dominated the management of General Motors during the period of Drucker's detailed analysis of the corporation, when it was manufacturing only defence equipment.*

worked in insurance, again as an analyst. During this time Drucker became reacquainted with Doris after a chance meeting on the escalators at Piccadilly Circus.

Drucker spent four years at a small London merchant bank, got disillusioned with economics after listening to John Maynard Keynes, and contributed freelance articles to American publications. In 1937 he married Doris and, sponsored by London financial papers, emigrated to the US, where he has lived and worked ever since, as journalist, author, speaker, consultant, and teacher (of both management and Oriental art). These occupations have a common link: writing. Drucker considers himself first and foremost as a writer, and least of all as an entrepreneur, for which he claims to have no talent whatsoever.

# Lucid writer, fluent speaker

As a writer Drucker has set new standards for lucidity and strength of argument, publishing many articles throughout his long career. As he approached 90, Drucker was still contributing to the Wall Street Journal and Harvard Business Review. The latter, in the March-April 1999 issue, published "Managing Oneself", an excerpt from Drucker's latest book, Management Challenges for the 21st Century. The excerpt is typical in its clarity and in the way in which Drucker astonishes his readers with an idea that, once studied, appears irrefutable. Witness this sentence: "There is one prerequisite for managing the second half of your life: you must begin doing so long before you enter it."

He has managed his own life with extraordinary skill and great mental agility. Every year or two, Drucker sets himself to master a new subject. He devours books and magazines, and has a memory so capacious that it appears inexhaustible. Its feats extend from remembering not only all his innumerable friends and their families but also volumes of historical and personal anecdote and the entire content of his lectures. Sitting on a chair or the edge of a table, he delivers lectures without notes or audio-visual aids, with total fluency, at a steady pace: he holds a watch, does not seem to look at it, but finishes dead on time.

# Key corporate study

Drucker's lecturing skills were obviously developed by his long career as a college lecturer, starting in America in 1939 and continuing all his life. During World War II, he worked part-time for the Board of Economic Warfare, and published his second book, *The Future of Industrial Man*, in 1942. It made a considerable impact, and a year later,

Drucker was invited by the vice-chairman of General Motors to make a study of the world's largest industrial corporation. As he wrote in his autobiography, *Adventures of a Bystander*, "It was literally for me the finger of providence".

The book resulting from his study of General Motors, entitled *Concept of the Corporation* and published in 1946, remains the only corporate study of lasting intellectual merit. It inevitably played a crucial role in developing Drucker's knowledge of management. Alfred P. Sloan Jr., then the head of GM, was a brilliant and wise practitioner from whom Drucker learnt a great deal. There were very few other sources of management wisdom at that time, certainly few in writing, and Drucker was able to combine his social ideas with the practical observation of what actually happens inside a profit-making organization.

## Discovering management

Despite the success of *Concept of the Corporation*, Drucker went through a fallow period as a book writer until 1950. *The New Society* was published that year, one of three works on social and political topics produced in the Fifties. But his discovery of management as a discipline in its own right, and as a major force in society, was germinating throughout the post-GM years. His thinking culminated in the publication in 1954 of *The Practice of Management*, which drew on a variety of sources: not only the GM experience, but his teaching of management at New York University, and his work as a consultant for major companies.

Drucker seldom refers directly to his consultancy work, which is individual (he has no organization), top-level, and highly prized. The two-way traffic between his ideas and his clients has been important, however, in shaping his thought. *The Practice of Management* was originally conceived as a guide for client managers, filling a huge gap. Since then management books have flooded forth, and he has contributed heavily to the flow: seven more books, ranging from the highly practical (*The Effective Executive*, 1966) to the wide-ranging, with the latest, *Management Challenges for the 21st Century*, published in 1999.

# Lifestyle preferences

Even though he has spent so many decades advising friends who run wealthy corporations, Drucker has adopted none of their lifestyle habits. He lives simply, does not have a secretary, and bangs out his own letters on a typewriter. In practical (though not literary) terms, the Information Revolution has passed him by. His globe-trotting, though, has always included as much cultural tourism as time allows, mostly organized around appearances that range from whole-day seminars to keynote speeches.

His schedule used to include annual trips to Europe and Japan. Drucker was among the first Western observers to spot the huge importance of the upsurge in Japanese competition and management expertise. In return, the Japanese were among the first to spot and adopt Drucker's most important teachings. In later years Drucker has preferred to stay at home in Claremont, near Los Angeles. When conference organizers have wanted him (and they do, all the time), then the new technology has come in handy, presenting him on screen via satellite. His hearing has worsened with advancing age, but his brilliance at understanding and interpretation is unimpaired. He remains the supreme master of his craft – which he did, after all, invent.

# 1

# Organizing for success in business

How decentralization contributed to the success of General Motors ● **Why the "self-governing community" is the ideal management system** ● The importance of giving workers a say in decisions ● **How people want to identify themselves with product and company, and to be held responsible for quality and performance** ● Understanding the importance of the "theory of the business" in winning success ● **The need to challenge every product, service, policy, and distribution channel every three years**

**D**rucker's reputation as a management expert got enormous impetus from his study of General Motors, commissioned by the directors in 1942 and most powerfully influenced by GM's creator, Alfred P. Sloan. The 33-year-old consultant and writer was given complete freedom during the 18 months that he spent studying the world's first manufacturing mega-corporation. Nor did GM seek any control over what he wrote afterwards about its methods and nature. The book Drucker produced, *Concept of the Corporation* (1946), made him the first, as well as the most insightful, writer to explore and explain the evolution of the business corporation as a key institution of society.

Drucker wished to generalize from the particular but GM was especially particular because of Sloan. An ascetic man, Sloan not only lived for the company, he lived in it, mostly sleeping in a little bedroom in the Detroit offices. The apartment on Fifth Avenue, New York, and the estate on Long Island were largely unused trappings for this childless, dedicated executive. He was atypical, not only of the top corporate managers of his time, but of all their successors. The company over which he reigned cannot be separated from Sloan's personality or his methods.

Consequently, GM was not the best possible source of generalizations. Drucker is no believer in the Great Man theory of history. Like Tolstoy, he is far more interested in the historical tides that carry away all men and women, great or small. But many of the key lessons that Drucker learnt from GM were taught by Sloan personally, rather than by the organization — for example, the sovereign importance of people decisions. "If we didn't spend four hours on placing a man and placing him right," taught Sloan, "we'd spend 400 hours cleaning up after our mistakes."

# Decentralized structure

**A**bove all, Sloan taught Drucker about decentralization. Drucker argues that, at GM, this principle had been taken far beyond its normal usage. "In over 20 years of work... Mr. Alfred P. Sloan Jr. has developed the concept of decentralization into a philosophy of industrial management and into a system of local self-government." Drucker was not, however, content to leave Sloan's principle as just a better way of organizing management within a major institution. "It is not a mere technique of management but an outline of a social order," he claimed.

By the standards of the day, Sloan gave his divisions (nearly 50 of them) great independence. Drucker estimated that all but 5 per cent of decisions came within the ambit of the individual divisions. This relative autonomy, however, was considerably limited by the powers retained by the centre, which made the 5 per cent very telling. The divisional managers had no control over prices, the cost of labour, the capital they employed, or the financial function. Moreover, the managers of these "profit centres" (a Drucker-invented term not then in use) were held highly accountable for their results.

That was one sterner aspect of the decentralization that Drucker described: the balance of delegation was tilted heavily towards the centre. Drucker observed that headquarters "refrains as much as possible from telling a division how to do its job; it only lays down what to do". However, by dictating what divisional managers at GM should be doing, central managers at GM paid little more than lip service to the freedom given to their subordinates under the decentralized regime; in reality, they were kept on a tight leash. You could look at Sloan's GM as the power structure of a control freak, or as a liberating mechanism.

# Corporation as human effort

**D**rucker leant towards the second alternative. GM, he wrote, had "realized its concept of decentralization sufficiently to obtain from it an overall pattern of behaviour and a basis for the successful solution of the most difficult concrete problems of economic life". He was particularly impressed by the impact of the decentralized structure on GM executives, whose placement was so important in Sloan's scheme. They were placed in jobs where, as relative youngsters, they could take responsibility without endangering the whole corporation, and, as they rose, so they broadened and applied their skills.

The very title of the book's section on decentralization gives away the author's main concern: "the corporation as human effort". Drucker was far less concerned with issues of efficiency or profitability (although he regarded profit as "the basis of all economic activity") than with the social and economic themes that dominate two-thirds of *Concept of the Corporation*. GM loomed large in these discussions, but only as evidence for the case: that such organizations were now America's "representative institution", that "the large mass-production plant is our social reality".

Drucker says that "only now have we realized" this truth, which is a modest way of saying that it was his discovery. He felt that the corporation was an engine with huge potential for good, which "has to carry the burden of our dreams". It was still, however, far from achieving the ideals enshrined in Drucker's dreams. GM's idea of employment was to achieve the highest production for the lowest possible cost. The role of the workers was to do as they were told, without complaint or individual contribution, as they served the monotonous, mindless machines of the assembly line in just as mindless a fashion.

**Helping hand**

*Established in 1908 by William C. Durant, General Motors had become the largest car manufacturer in the US long before 1953, when this young apprentice was being taught his trade.*

# Self-governing plant community

This attitude to employees was anathema to Drucker who, even at this extremely early date, was preaching "empowerment". He thought GM could and should create "the self-governing plant community", whose members would contribute to improving their work and would take pride in what they were doing. Such an approach would inevitably mean scrapping the assembly line, which Drucker criticized on both economic and human grounds. The line moved at the pace of the slowest worker, nobody produced a finished product, and – in his view – the monotony was literally counter-productive. Needless to say, the argument fell on stony ground at GM, over whom Drucker believed he had no influence whatsoever.

But any other major corporation would have reacted similarly. This was the age of economies of scale. Giants like General Motors built huge plants to milk these economies. Profitability hinged on using these industrial mammoths to the highest possible capacity, reducing operations to repetitive tasks, and relying as little as possible on variable human skills, as opposed to machine-like consistency. Drucker clearly recognized this fact of economic life: "... we know today that in modern industrial production, particularly in modern mass production, the small unit is not only inefficient, it cannot produce at all".

Not surprisingly, this made the author sound like an advocate of the large corporation, even though he believed the "small unit" was far better placed to give the worker economic dignity. But smallness was incompatible, not only with productivity, but with the heroic status Drucker wished the corporation to assume. Unfortunately, neither GM nor any other giant wanted to assume the mantle of leading the US into a new industrial order, especially given the forms of leadership Drucker had in mind.

Drucker wanted to humanize the treatment of workers, and to give them a say in workplace decisions. He wanted the long-term workers to have a guaranteed annual wage. This meant that their livelihoods would not be destroyed

**"Management is about human beings. Its task is to make people capable of joint performance, to make their strengths effective and their weaknesses irrelevant. This is what organization is all about, and it is the reason that management is the... determining factor."** *The New Realities*

by downturns in the market. In fact, this was a brilliant perception, both for the company and society. As Drucker argued, guaranteed pay would maintain the purchasing power of workers during a recession. It would also retain and motivate the workers, no longer treated as expendable by the management.

Unfortunately, GM's labour troubles at the end of World War II made it impossible for its management (including Sloan) to listen sympathetically to a case for better treatment of the employees. In nature, Drucker's arguments were perilously close to those of Walter Reuther, the forceful head of the United Auto Workers Union, and GM's sworn enemy. As so often, Drucker was ahead of his time, both in preaching empowerment and in his ideas on wages: a long time later the guaranteed wage was adopted by the corporation. In fact, under "Engine" Charlie Wilson, Sloan's successor, Drucker was used as a consultant on labour matters.

# Corporation as pillar of society

Wilson was the source of a famous misquotation: "What's good for General Motors is good for America." He actually said, "What's good for America is good for General Motors, and vice versa" (1953), which is not the same thing at all. The accurate quote plainly, if clumsily, reflects Drucker's view of the corporation as a pillar of the wider society. Presumably under Drucker's influence, Wilson also enquired into employees' opinions, which turned out to include a desire to help improve their jobs. Neither union boss Reuther nor other GM managers thought much of this concept. "Managers should manage and workers work", maintained Reuther.

That didn't square at all with Wilson's findings, which, according to Drucker, showed that employees truly wanted "to identify themselves with product and company and to be held responsible for quality and performance". This was the desire that became the seed for the post-war rebirth of Japanese management (see p. 24) and its much later Western versions. But at GM, Drucker's study, which enormously influenced the behaviour of other corporations worldwide, led only to Sloan's book, *My Years at General Motors* (1963). Intended as a response, to set the record straight, Sloan's book neither mentions Drucker nor pays any great attention to the period of his study: a war in which GM made only defence equipment.

**Organizational genius**
*General Motors owed much of its enormous success to Alfred P. Sloan (1875–1966), who restructured the corporation in the early 1920s. He became president in 1924 and chairman in 1937.*

Drucker, on the other hand, enormously values Sloan's achievement, both as a manager who ruled by moral authority and as a superb organizer. As Drucker wrote in 1994, "GM had an even more powerful, and successful, theory of the business than IBM.... The company did not have one setback in 70 years – a record unmatched in business history. GM's theory combined, in one seamless web, assumptions about markets and customers with assumptions about core competencies and organizational structure." And that was predominantly Sloan's work.

# Theory of the business

According to Drucker, every organization, "whether a business or not", has a "theory of the business". Sounding very close to "concept of the corporation", "theory of the business" sums up the "assumptions on which the organization has been built and is being run". The conventional view is that these assumptions, especially in large corporations, ossify, and management then becomes "bureaucratic, sluggish, or arrogant". The trio of adjectives certainly seemed to explain what happened to GM in the early 1980s, years "in which GM's main business, passenger automobiles, seemed almost paralyzed". Yet GM in the same period had two great successes with expensive acquisitions, Hughes Aircraft and EDS, which hardly fits the adjectives.

"What can explain", asks Drucker, "the fact that... the policies, practices, and behaviours that worked for decades – and in the case of GM are still working well when applied to something new and different – no longer work for the organization in which and for which they were developed?" His answer is that the car market had changed, so that GM's basic plan, to have massively long runs of unchanged models aimed at each income segment, ceased to fit. As a result Sloan's entire divisional structure and production system were undermined: "GM knew all this but simply could not believe it.... Instead, the company tried to patch things over... [which] only confused the customer, the dealer, and the employees and management of GM itself."

Drucker explains that every "theory of the business" has three parts. "First, there are assumptions about the environment of the organization.... Second, there are assumptions about the specific mission of the organization.... Third, there are assumptions about the core competencies needed to accomplish the organization's mission." A company does not arrive at a theory overnight. "It usually takes years of hard work, thinking, and experimenting to a reach a clear, consistent, and valid theory of the business."

But what makes this theory valid? Drucker lays down four conditions:

- The assumptions about the environment, mission, and core competencies must fit reality.
- The assumptions in all three areas have to fit one another.
- The theory of the business must be known and understood throughout the organization.
- The theory of the business has to be tested constantly and altered if necessary.

Drucker points out in *Managing in a Time of Great Change* (1995) that GM was especially strong on the second point. "Its assumptions about the market and about the optimum manufacturing process were a perfect fit. GM decided in the mid-1920s that it also required new and as-yet-unheard-of core competencies: financial control of the manufacturing process and a theory of capital allocations. As a result, GM invented modern cost-accounting and the first rational capital-allocation process."

## Maintaining a valid theory

If any of the assumptions, let alone all of them, become falsified, the theory of the business must collapse. How does an organization stop that happening? "There are only two preventive measures," asserts Drucker. The first he calls "abandonment", by which he means that: "Every three years, an organization should challenge every product, every service, every policy, every distribution channel with the question, 'If we were not in it already, would we be going into it now?'"

This approach forces the company to ask the following crucial questions: "Why didn't this work, even though it looked so promising when we went into it five years ago? Is it because we made a mistake? Is it because we did the wrong things? Or is it because the right things didn't work?"

The second preventive measure "is to study what goes on outside the business, and especially to study non-customers". Drucker points out that, although "knowing as much as possible about one's customers" is important, "the first signs of fundamental change rarely appear within one's own organization or among one's own customers". The people who are *not* buying from you "almost always" reveal those first signs, to which, Drucker emphasizes, managers must pay acute attention. They should also bear in mind that a "theory of the business always becomes obsolete when an organization attains its original objectives".

Another "sure sign of crisis" for any company is rapid growth. "Any organization that doubles or triples its size within a fairly short period of time has necessarily outgrown its theory," he observes. In these circumstances, to "continue in health, let alone grow, the organization has to ask itself again the questions about its environment, mission, and core competencies". Rapid growth at least was rarely GM's problem. The corporation did, however, ignore "two more clear signals that an organization's theory of the business is no longer valid".

# Unexpected success and failure

One of these signals is "unexpected success – whether one's own or a competitor's. The other is unexpected failure – again, whether one's own or a competitor's". GM provides a model, or rather a warning, on both counts. Drucker maintains, for example, that "had it paid attention to the success [in minivans] of its weaker competitor, Chrysler, GM might have realized much earlier that its assumptions about both its market and its core competencies were no longer valid". In fact, light trucks, and therefore potentially minivans, were an area in which GM might have expected to dominate.

As for unexpected failure, none was more unexpected or more devastating than the collapse of GM's market share before the post-war onslaughts of the Japanese – who had adopted Drucker's ideas concerning empowerment, set out in *Concept of the Corporation*, and ignored by GM, with great enthusiasm. "My popularity in Japan", wrote Drucker, "where I am credited with substantial responsibility for the emergence of the country as a major economic power and for the performance and productivity of its industry, goes back to *Concept of the Corporation*, which was almost immediately translated into Japanese, eagerly read and applied."

The irony is unmistakeable. A book extolling the virtues of GM at its peak became the text for many Japanese manufacturers, above all Toyota, whose managers did much to topple Sloan's creation from its eminence. This achievement testifies less to GM's weaknesses than to the abiding strength of Drucker's ideas about corporate organization.

## Ideas into action

- Spend all the time you need on making decisions that affect people.

- Make sure that everybody understands what your business is really about.

- Study what is going on outside the business, and among customers and non-customers.

- If the business is growing fast, question your assumptions all over again.

- Look out for and learn from unexpected success – your own and others'.

- Do exactly the same with unexpected failure, especially your own.

# The meeting with General Motors

Drucker's epochal work, *Concept of the Corporation*, was an opportunity waiting to happen. He had made several unsuccessful attempts to get inside a major organization when the call from GM came "out of the blue" in 1942.

**D**rucker had a guinea pig, the biggest in the world, for establishing and exploring the theory of organizations. The only catch was GM itself: a business making profits, run by corporate managers, about whose work Drucker was ignorant.

Drucker found that there was almost no literature on the management and structure of large businesses and set out to repair the omission. GM originally wanted a study for internal eyes only, but Drucker held that employees would not trust or confide in him unless he was seen as impartial and independent from top management. It was agreed that Drucker should instead write an independent book, which GM would correct only for factual error.

## A free hand

The key to the analysis of GM was Alfred P. Sloan, the man who had assembled GM from separate automobile manufacturers, and who dominated its management with a style that was by no means domineering. For example, although he objected to the Drucker project, he let himself be outvoted. He then told Drucker, "I shall not tell you what to write, what to study, or what conclusions to come to…. My only instruction to you is to put down what you think is right…. Don't you worry about our reactions."

## Unacceptable views

As it happened, the management's reactions were decidedly unfavourable. The book came out in 1946 when GM was experiencing severe labour troubles, which helped to make Drucker's conclusions unacceptable. For example, he proposed paying a guaranteed annual wage, which was also sought by the union, and argued for more worker involvement in decision making (see p. 58). Sloan had originally told Drucker not to concern himself "with the compromises that might be needed" to make his recommendations acceptable. Now he repudiated the book, and

26

> **"Sloan has developed the concept of decentralization into a philosophy of industrial management and into a system of local self-government. It is… an outline of a social order."**
> *Concept of the Corporation*

wrote his own, *My Years with General Motors*, itself a management classic, almost as a rebuttal.

The circumstances for Drucker's 18 months of research were not ideal. As it was wartime, GM was making no cars, only defence equipment, such as tanks, aircraft, and machine guns. The operation of the company as a marketing machine or as a producer of consumer goods was therefore outside his scan. Also, war workers tend to have high morale, making GM's unsympathetic and counter-productive management of its workforce hard to uncover. His vision of GM's post-war leadership of industrial society was not founded in reality, nor shared by the corporation's leaders.

For all that, Drucker stayed in close contact with GM, and some of the credit he won for developing the concept of a benevolent, socially responsible capitalist organization, rubbed off on the corporation. And the day came when its workers did receive a guaranteed annual wage.

OUTPUT GRAPHS FOR 16 ON DEVICES

PELLET SORT    PVC    MOUNT

BOND    BOND CHECK

# 2

# The art of management in practice

Why 90 per cent of management concerns are shared by all organizations ● **Making the strengths and knowledge of each individual more productive** ● Founding the business on customer values and customer decisions ● **The five basic elements in the work of the manager** ● The three key questions that govern true delegation ● **Using the Feedback Analysis to compare expectation with results and improve performance** ● How to use new measurements to achieve improved performance from everyone

**D**rucker is a humanist who upholds the traditional liberal values of the European intelligentsia. That he should also be the leading exponent of management theory is no paradox. He stresses that, without management, organizations cannot meet the social purposes that transcend them. He calls management a "liberal art", not a science. Here there is a paradox, since many of the writers and teachers who spread the concept of "scientific management" were following in Drucker's footsteps. That is because his footsteps are unavoidable.

Starting in 1954 with *The Practice of Management* (still considered his greatest contribution by some experts), Drucker on his own account invented his subject. He observes that hardly anything on management, as opposed to subjects like selling, advertising, and manufacturing, existed before the book appeared. He reckoned that even people in business "often do not know what their management does and what it is supposed to be doing, how it acts and why, whether it does a good job or not", so Drucker set out to fill this enormous gap, combining theory with eminently practical advice.

His approach has set him at odds with the vast majority of business management academics (although he has long been such an academic himself). He criticizes their excessive focus on academic respectability. Because they were long scorned by other university faculties, the business schools have been eager to prove their true, rigorous academic credentials. That focus ignores Drucker's proposition that management is art rather than science. To Drucker, management is "an integrating discipline of human values and conduct, of social order and intellectual inquiry". It is an art that "feeds off economics, psychology, mathematics, political theory, history, and philosophy".

# The scope of management

**M**ost managers would be amazed, if flattered, to learn that this description defines their daily activity. The false scientists in the business schools are equally far from practising what Drucker preaches. Most of the curricula lay heavy stress on financial analysis and other mathematical disciplines. He regards this approach as another excess, which confuses management with "quantification". Not surprisingly, given his early statistical background, Drucker's own teaching does emphasize the importance of establishing the numerical and financial facts. But that is a foundation of managing, not the whole of management.

Few managers would make as great claims for their discipline as Drucker does on their behalf. They think of their art (Drucker has also called it a "social science") as specifically *business* management. Drucker finds this definition far too narrow. He recognizes that there are differences between managing "a chain of retail stores and managing a Catholic diocese (although amazingly fewer than either chain stores or bishops believe)". He does not regard these differences as significant.

The "greatest differences" are in the terms that individual organizations use. "Otherwise the differences are mainly in application rather than in principles," Drucker asserts. He goes on to argue that all executives in all organizations spend about the same amount of time on people problems: "and the people problems are nearly always the same". He puts the "generic" element of management at a huge 90 per cent of the whole. That leaves very little that "has to be fitted to the organization's specific mission, its specific culture, its specific history, and its specific vocabulary". The argument is sweeping, probably too sweeping, but it sets the stage for the following large claim: "management is the specific and distinguishing organ of any and all organizations".

This is the latest statement (taken from *Management Challenges for the 21st Century*, 1999) of a position Drucker has held since the 1950s. At that time, he applied the word "organ" in a quasi-medical sense: "management is an organ, and organs can only be defined through their function". This "specific organ of the business enterprise", in author Jack Beatty's summary, has three functions: to manage a business, to manage managers, and to manage worker and work. Today, however, Drucker argues that "one does not 'manage' people. The task is to lead people. And the goal is to make productive the specific strengths and knowledge of each individual." That is a high internal ambition.

# Importance of the customer

As an "organ of society" the "business enterprise" has an ultimate purpose outside itself. Drucker maintains, "There is only one valid definition of business purpose: to create a customer." He regards this definition as one of his crucial ideas. It has had an incalculable influence on the preaching and practice of management, culminating in today's pursuit of "customer focus" (or putting the customer first), and in the contemporary ideal of the "customer-centric" business, organized from beginning to end around customer satisfaction.

In one way or another, the customer theme runs through all Drucker's work, from *Concept of the Corporation* right up to the present day. "The foundations have to be customer values and customer decisions," he argues. "It is with those that management policy and management strategy increasingly will have to start." It follows logically from this that the customer must also be the starting point for the actual practice of management.

## What management does

**D**rucker has explored the practice of management with unfailing vigour and insight since the 1950s. In 1973, he produced *Management: Tasks, Responsibilities, Practices*, which became a bestselling must for aspiring Masters of Business Administration. It summarizes the three decades of theorizing and practical observation that began when he entered the gates of General Motors. In the book Drucker identifies five basic functions of a manager.

"A manager, in the first place, sets objectives. He determines what the objectives should be. He determines what the goals in each area of objectives should be. He decides what has to be done to reach these objectives. He makes the objectives effective by communicating them to the people whose performance is needed to attain them.

"Second, a manager organizes. He analyzes the activities, decisions, and relations needed. He classifies the work. He divides it into manageable activities and further divides the activities into manageable jobs. He groups these units and jobs into an organization structure. He selects people for the management of these units and for the jobs to be done.

"Next, a manager motivates and communicates. He makes a team out of the people that are responsible for various jobs. He does that through the practices with which he works. He does it in his own relations to the men with whom he works. He does it through his

**Communicating with individual units**

*A manager should provide team members with the information they require to do a good job, communicating with them frequently, and giving them clear guidelines on the results that are expected.*

'people decisions' on pay, placement, and promotion. And he does it through constant communication, to and from his subordinates, to and from his superior, and to and from his colleagues.

"The fourth basic element in the work of the manager is measurement. The manager establishes yardsticks – and few factors are as important to the performance of the organization and every man in it. He sees to it that each man has measurements available to him which are focused on the performance of the whole organization and which, at the same time, focus on the work of the individual and help him do it. He analyzes, appraises, and interprets performance. As in all other areas of his work, he communicates the meaning of the measurements and their findings to his subordinates, to his superiors, and to colleagues.

"Finally, a manager develops people, including himself."

# Hero chief executives

Of all those self-developers, the most important is the person at the top. Carrying out all of the first four duties for a major corporation is an heroic task, and articles in the media suggest that top management heroes duly abound. But Drucker believes that the hero chief executive (a type whose hype recurs through thick and thin, boom and bust) exceeds the normal limits of human capacity. Four quite different types of person are required to fulfil the role of chief executive successfully: thought man, action man, people man, and front man.

According to Drucker, "those four temperaments are almost never found in one person. The one-man top management job is a major reason why businesses fail to grow." One of the exceptions to his rule was the very man who led General Motors, the company whose study opened the doors to Drucker's thoughts on the practice of management – Alfred P. Sloan. Sloan, however, was a practising manager who reduced management to two simple ideas: incentive compensation and "decentralization with coordinated control". The latter provided opportunity, the former produced motivation.

**"I have held from the beginning that management has to be a discipline, an organized body of knowledge that can be learned..."** *The Frontiers of Management*

# Effective self-management

Sloan was also extremely efficient at a critical aspect of every manager's job: managing oneself. Drucker has always paid close attention to the individual manager's work. His most famous formulation in this regard forms the basis of the delegation without which decentralization cannot work. He suggests that every manager should periodically ask themselves the following three key questions:

■ What am I doing that does not need to be done at all?
■ What am I doing that can be done by somebody else?
■ What am I doing that only I can do?

This simple and elegant set of questions goes to the heart of the use of time and the employment of talents – your own and other people's. Drucker has developed his thinking about self-management to keep in step with the rise of the knowledge worker (see p. 93), which imposes "drastically new demands" on individuals. They have to ask:

■ Who am I?
■ What are my strengths?
■ How do I work?
■ Where do I belong?
■ What is my contribution?

There is only one way to answer the first three of these five questions: the Feedback Analysis. "Whenever one makes a key decision, and whenever one does a key action, one writes down what one expects to happen. And nine months or 12 months later one then feeds back from results to expectations. And every time I do it I am surprised. And so is everybody who has ever done this." Using the results of the Feedback Analysis, managers concentrate on using and improving their revealed strengths.

Managers must also take "relationship responsibility", which Drucker calls an "absolute necessity. It is a duty". He points out that "organizations are no longer built on force. They are built on trust". Personality conflicts arise mostly because "one person does not know what the other person does", or how that is done, or its contribution, or the expected results. The manager "owes relationship responsibility to everyone with whom one works, on whose work one depends, and who in turn depends on one's work."

# Measuring performance

In this new world of the knowledge worker, Drucker argues, new measures are also required. The old methods of accountancy, for example, were geared to an economy that is fast vanishing. You cannot measure a knowledge company by the same criteria as one producing nuts and bolts. He has said that "performance will have to be defined non-financially so as to be meaningful to knowledge workers and to generate commitment from them".

He calls traditional measures "an X-ray of the enterprise's skeleton", but points out that "the diseases we most commonly die from... do not show up in a skeletal X-ray". In the same way: "... a loss of market standing or a failure to innovate does not register in the accountant's figures until the damage has been done. We need new measurements — call them 'a business audit' — to give us effective business control."

Increasingly, "result control" is obtained from "activity-based costing" which recognizes that the "cost that matters for competitiveness and profitability is the cost of the total process", and includes the costs of "not doing" (such as machine downtime). Going further, a company has to know the costs of its "entire economic chain", going outside the company to determine the final cost to the customer. Drucker strongly advocates "price-led costing", in which companies work back from what the customer is prepared to pay.

### Customer focus
*Creating a customer, says Drucker, is the only "valid definition of business purpose": therefore customer values and decisions are the starting points for policy and strategy.*

# The diagnostic toolkit

He adds, however, that "enterprises are paid to create wealth". That requires four sets of diagnostic tools which together "constitute the executive's toolkit for managing the current business". They are:

- Foundation information
- Productivity information
- Competence information
- Resource-allocation information

Foundation information refers to familiar measures like cashflow, sales, and various ratios, which conventional businesses have long used. If they are normal, fine; abnormality indicates "a problem that needs to be identified and treated". Productivity information looks at the productivity of key resources, including labour – with manual labour currently much easier to measure than knowledge and service work. Drucker stresses that you also need measures like "economic value-added analysis" to demonstrate that a business is earning more than its capital costs, together with "benchmarking" to show that its performance is as good as or better than the best competition.

With competence information, Drucker ventures on less well-trodden ground. How do you measure "core competencies" like the Japanese genius at miniaturizing electronic components? "Every organization... needs one core competence: innovation," he asserts. How, again, do you measure performance in this critical area? Unusually, Drucker has no answers, only questions such as: "How many of the truly important innovation opportunities did we miss? Why? Because we did not see them? Or because we saw them but dismissed them?" Much of this, he admits, "is assessment rather than measurement" – an omission that he would plainly like to rectify.

With resource-allocation information, Drucker is on home ground. He long ago spotted that none of the traditional measures of capital employment – return on investment, payback period, cashflow, or discounted present value – was enough on its own. "To understand a proposed investment, a company needs to look at all four", and to ask two key questions that do not figure in most capital appropriation processes:

■ What will happen if the investment fails to produce the promised results? Would it seriously hurt the company?
■ If the investment is successful, especially more so than we expect, what will it commit us to?

Drucker adds that "there is no better way to improve an organization's performance than to measure the results of capital spending against the promises and expectations that led to its authorizations". Capital, however, is only one key resource of the organization. "The scarcest resources are performing people." He calls for "placement" of people with specific expectations as to what the appointee should achieve and with systematic appraisal of the outcome. Again, although Drucker is certain about the end (to allocate human resources "as purposefully and thoughtfully" as capital), he is less sure about the means.

In any case, businesses need to measure the future as well as the present. "Strategy has to be based on information about markets, customers, and non-customers" and about technology, finance, and the "changing world" outside. "Inside an organization there are only cost centres. The only profit centre is a customer whose cheque has not bounced." Drucker notes the first efforts to organize "business intelligence", information about actual and potential competitors worldwide. But here, as elsewhere, he perceives a serious lag and challenge. "The majority of enterprises have yet to start the job," he observes.

Once managers know what information they need for their work and what information they owe to others, they can develop methods to turn "the chaos of data" into "organized and focused information". With that in hand, they can begin to exploit the "most valuable assets of a 21st-century institution: its knowledge workers and their productivity".

## Ideas into action

- Make sure you communicate clearly and often with colleagues, superiors, and subordinates.

- Do the Feedback Analysis as a matter of course to build on your strengths.

- Gain really effective control by conducting a comprehensive "business audit".

- Work back to costs from what customers are prepared to pay.

- Look at several measures of capital employment – not just one.

- Have specific expectations for people's performance and appraise it systematically.

- Develop "business intelligence" about actual and potential competitors worldwide.

# The invention of management

Jack Beatty, in *The World According to Drucker* (1998), dates Peter Drucker's defining moment as a management author precisely: "On or about November 6, 1954, Peter Drucker invented management."

The date refers to the publication of *The Practice of Management*, and the author has no doubts about its importance. "When I published *The Practice of Management*, that book made it possible for people to learn how to manage, something that up until then only a few geniuses seemed able to do, and nobody could replicate it."

Drucker has no doubt that "management" was his brainchild. An interview with Warren Bennis in May 1982, titled "The Invention of Management", includes an account of a visit to one Harry Hopf, who was supposed to have "the biggest management library in the world. The only one". Among the "thousands and thousands of volumes", however, there were only six about management. Of these Drucker found that half "weren't quite management. So practically nothing existed". As his host explained: "The rest are all about insurance, selling, advertising, and manufacturing." None of these activities can be

conducted without "managing". They all need recruitment, remuneration policies, decision taking, planning, strategies, and many other activities that plainly come under the heading of management. So what exactly had Drucker "invented"?

## Key book

To all intents and purposes Drucker invented the management book. There were business books and books on various techniques available at the time. Before Drucker even visited General Motors, for instance, the great entrepreneur Forrest Mars was using the performance measurement techniques presented in *Higher Control in Management* by a little-known Briton, T. G. Rose.

There were plenty of other experts and expert authors – including management consultants. None of these contributed more than James O. McKinsey, who was a pioneer of scientific management 29 years before Drucker's "invention". Three

**"You can't do carpentry, you know, if you only have a saw, or only a hammer, or you never heard of a pair of pliers. It's when you put all those tools into one kit that you invent."** *The Frontiers of Management*

years before that, the *Harvard Business Review* published its first issue. So management journalism also existed, as did the academic faculties from which the *Harvard Business Review* sprang. Its founder, the dean of the Harvard Business School, specifically wanted the journal to help "improve the practice of management". Drucker brought together all these strands.

In *The Practice of Management* Drucker took on board the pioneering of the consultants, who mostly developed their ideas from financial accounting; the organizational feats of men like Sloan; the gradual build-up of academic knowledge and teaching; the body of expertise on subjects ranging from marketing to mass production; and the experience of numberless managers in myriad firms. He embraced all this in an intellectual framework that explained to managers what they were doing and why – and, even more important, told them what they should do.

# Managing effectively

*everal decades of practical observation led Drucker to conclude that there are five essential functions that combine to form the basis of every manager's job. Aim to improve your skills in each of these five areas, and assess your progress throughout the learning process.*

| The Five Functions of a Manager | | | | |
|---|---|---|---|---|
| **1** Setting objectives | **2** Organizing the group | **3** Motivating and communicating | **4** Measuring performance | **5** Developing people |

**Effectiveness versus efficiency**

Drucker stresses the vital distinction between effectiveness (doing the right thing) and efficiency (doing things right). For each of the five functions of a manager, ask yourself these two key questions:

■ Am I truly effective?

■ Or am I merely efficient?

To quantify the results, do a simple exercise. Set out two columns headed "Effective" and "Efficient" on a piece of paper, and write the five functions down the side. Against each function list the activities involved. For each function mark yourself out of 10 for effectiveness (doing the right thing) and for efficiency (doing things right).

**Assessing your performance**

Add up your score and compare it with the analysis below. A perfect total of 100 is unlikely. There is always a gap between actual performance and perfection – your score will show how far you have to go. Next, look at the balance between the effectiveness and efficiency scores. This is as important as your total; doing the right things badly and the wrong things well are both ineffective. Now concentrate on developing all five skills in the sections that follow.

| Analysis |
|---|
| ■ 35 or below: your performance is inadequate. Act fast to improve your efficiency and effectiveness. |
| ■ 35–70: your performance is average to good, but requires improvement. |
| ■ 75 or above: you are efficient and effective, but cannot afford to relax. |

PETER DRUCKER

# 1 Setting objectives

Setting objectives involves a continuous process of research and decision-making. Ensure that your personal objectives and those of your job (at the unit and organizational levels) are the same.

## Self-knowledge

Knowledge of yourself and your unit is a vital starting point in setting objectives. To discover how your strengths contribute to the organization's objectives, Drucker advocates asking five questions. Ask them, not only about yourself, but about your unit. The answers will identify what changes must be made in order to get the results you expect. The next step is to undertake a Feedback Analysis to compare actual results with expectations.

| Assess Yourself | Assess Your Unit |
|---|---|
| Who am I? | What is its role? |
| What are my strengths? | What are its resources? |
| How do I work? | How does it function? |
| Where do I belong? | What is my function within it? |
| What is my contribution? | What are the functions of others? |

**Do the Feedback Analysis**

Whenever you take a key decision or action, write down what you expect to happen.

Review results at regular intervals, and compare them with expectations.

Use this feedback as a guide and goad to reinforce strengths and eliminate weaknesses.

## Applying the Feedback Analysis

Carry out the Feedback Analysis as often as you feel necessary, and ask the people who work for you to do likewise. The results of each analysis will provide a strong foundation for the next round of setting objectives, both for you and your unit.

# 2 Organizing the group

Unless the way in which your unit, or group, is organized is suitable for its purposes and the people in it, failure will result. Once you have set the objectives (see p. 45), provide the human resources needed to meet them, and ensure that they are effectively deployed.

### Defining work

In the well-organized group, nobody does anything superfluous, and the leader only does the tasks that nobody else can do. To help you define and allot tasks, including your own, ask yourself three of Drucker's most penetrating questions:

■ What am I doing that does not need to be done at all?
■ What am I doing that can be done by somebody else?
■ What am I doing that only I can do?

### Delegating tasks

Always drop unnecessary work altogether. Necessary tasks that you do not need to do should be delegated. Delegation itself – finding the right person and giving them the right work – is the one task that you cannot delegate. Resist the temptation to keep tasks to yourself as a means of control or, worse, a demonstration of power. You should be interested in authority, but only in the authority of expertise – that is, your delegates (and your peers) follow your lead because you are good at your job. Resist, too, delegating in a haphazard fashion. Always ensure that your choice of delegate is based on a fair and objective assesment of his or her skills and abilities in relation to the requirements of the task.

PETER DRUCKER

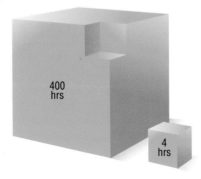

400 hrs

4 hrs

### Saving time

*Alfred P. Sloan, the GM executive who gave Drucker masterclasses in management, said of selection: "If we didn't spend four hours on placing a man and placing him right, we'd spend 400 hours cleaning up after our mistakes."*

# 3 Motivating and communicating

The good motivator motivates people to motivate themselves. Rather than relying on your powers (exhortation, reward, or punishment, for example) to provide a spur, use the powers within people.

## Sharing motivation

Ideally, those who work for you share your motivation. To find out if they do, both as individuals and as a group, ask yourself:

■ Do they identify themselves with the organization and their own group?

■ Do they identify themselves with its products and/or services?

■ Do they accept individual and group responsibility for the quality and performance of their work?

The more positive the answers, the stronger the foundations for teamwork and for leadership, which is about your personal example, how you conduct your relationships with your people, and the decisions you make on the all-important Three Ps.

| The Three Ps | | |
|:---:|:---:|:---:|
| **1 Pay** | **2 Placement** | **3 Promotion** |

## A two-way relationship

Have clear reasons for your decisions on the Three Ps, and always communicate these reasons to everybody concerned. Ask yourself:

■ What information do I owe to the people with whom I work and on whom I depend?

■ In what form?

■ And in what time frame?

Make sure that you use the answers to these questions as the basis for your communications. Do not think of communication as a separate and periodic task. Use every means available to let everyone working with you know your plans and your reasons. Remember that communication is two-way, so ensure that the channels are fully open to others so that they can give you the information you need. That includes, as a vital matter, feedback to make certain that communication has become understanding and consensus.

#  Measuring performance

In most companies, the measuring of performance is dominated by financial numbers – sales figures, cash flow, and profit – giving a limited, one-dimensional picture of progress. To obtain a clear and wide-ranging view of performance levels, always use the greatest variety of indicators possible.

## The whole picture

Write down a list of the things you need to know and the issues you need to manage in order to perform your job effectively. Then write beside them the indicators that will measure that effectiveness. The following are likely to appear as entries on your list:

- Market share
- Quality
- Innovation
- Competitiveness
- Customer satisfaction
- Employee morale
- Cost of waste
- Use of capital
- Productivity

Although all of these contribute to the outcome in cashflow and profits, none can be measured by either figure. Think very carefully about each indicator you choose. Take market share: the crude division of total cash sales will be misleading, for example, if your unit sales are disproportionately low (you may be over-pricing) or high (you may be buying market share). You need to look at both unit sales and cash share to get a comprehensive and accurate picture of your overall performance. Ensure that all members of a team are involved in measuring performance to keep everyone focused on raising standards across the board.

PETER DRUCKER

---

### Measuring in the Round

The use of capital is a classic Drucker example of measuring performance in the round. Do not take the usual one-dimensional view of profits as a percentage of capital employed. To measure a potential investment, answer six questions. Once the investment has been made, ask how the outcome compared with expectations.

- How long will it take for profits to pay back the investment?
- When will the cash stop flowing out and start returning?
- Do we really have to make this investment?

- What is the return on investment?
- Is that return comfortably above the true cost of the capital invested?
- Looking ahead, and allowing for interest rates, what is the future pay-off worth in today's values?

# 5 Developing yourself and others

You have a responsibility, what Drucker calls a "relationship responsibility", for those with whom you work. Trust and know your colleagues. This is a moral responsibility that you owe to everybody, for you depend on their work as they depend on yours.

## Test your knowledge

Carrying out this responsibility develops the abilities of manager and managed alike. Consider these questions:

- Do I know what everybody else does?
- Do I know how they perform?
- Do I know what they contribute and what results are expected?
- Do I trust the people I work with?
- Do I treat each of them as individuals?
- Do I know their strengths?

Work towards a positive answer to each of them.

## Focus on strengths

Developing people starts with the self. Do the Feedback Analysis (see p. 45) to show you where your strengths and weaknesses lie. Based on this information, form a six-step action plan:

| Six-Step Action Plan |
| :---: |
| **1** Identify your strengths |
| **2** Improve your strengths |
| **3** Increase your knowledge |
| **4** Eliminate bad habits |
| **5** Practice good manners |
| **6** Avoid weak areas |

Drucker advises that you should concentrate on your strengths and waste as little effort as possible on improving areas of low competence. Ask everyone who works for you to adopt an action plan. With your help, it will take them forward – and you with them.

# 3

# Managing by objectives & self-control

The eight key areas where managers must pursue clear objectives ● **Why managers must master five basic functions to be effective** ● Producing results on the outside − in the market and the economy ● **Creating strategy that is customer-focused, entrepreneurial, market-leading, innovative, and tied to decisive opportunities** ● The essential principles of empowerment ● **Getting the right music from the managerial orchestra** ● How to make the right decisions about people − including yourself

Unlike other management writers, Drucker has rarely been identified with particular cure-all remedies. In the hands of others, the panacea approach has been used as a Unique Selling Proposition, the weapon with which to establish an academic reputation, or a rich consultancy practice, or (not infrequently) both. Drucker's sceptical turn of mind subjects cults and bogus claims to withering analysis. Yet he himself has been closely identified with one of the longest-lasting and most widely accepted wonder techniques of all: Management by Objectives (MBO).

Jack Beatty, in *The World According to Drucker*, calls MBO "Drucker's signature management concept". In *The Witch Doctors* (1996), John Micklethwait and Adrian Wooldridge of *The Economist* say that "Drucker invented" MBO, which they call "one of the rational school of management's most successful products". They do not, however, define the product, and seem to confuse Drucker's prime and unarguable insight — that management must set and have clear objectives — with what MBO became, a highly arguable system of command and control. While the setting of objectives is essential for an effective company, management by objectives is not.

# Integrated management system

The MBO technique is only one way of seeking to control, co-ordinate, and motivate managers — and it is not necessarily the best. Starting from the top of a company, the six stages of MBO are:

■ Define corporate objectives at board level.
■ Analyze management tasks and devise formal job

specifications, which allocate responsibilities and decisions to individual managers.
- Set performance standards.
- Agree and set specific objectives.
- Align individual targets with corporate objectives.
- Establish a management information system to monitor achievements against objectives.

Support for all six elements – sometimes strong support – can be found in Drucker's writings. The trouble comes when the six elements are combined to comprise a system of management. The complete MBO system is supposed to get managers off and running, busily acting to implement and achieve their plans, which automatically achieve those of the organization. The review mechanism enables bosses to make sure that their managers are performing as they should – especially in the "key result areas" that are a strong feature of MBO.

### Determining company objectives
*For MBO to be effective, individual managers must understand the specific objectives of their job and how those objectives fit in with the overall company objectives set by the board of directors.*

# Performing in key result areas

In his book *The Practice of Management* (1954), Drucker names eight of the key result areas where managers need, above all, to pursue clear objectives:

- Marketing
- Innovation
- Human organization
- Financial resources

- Physical resources
- Productivity
- Social responsibility
- Profit requirements

In reality MBO, as applied in hundreds of companies, has concentrated far more on achieving objectives in the last of these key areas – profit – than in any other area. The bottom line figures largely in salary review, which is important in the MBO system, along with matters such as management development and career progression. Obviously, these activities take place in companies that have no MBO system or anything like it. Obviously, too, you cannot run a proper budget system without setting objectives, and you cannot run MBO without proper budgeting.

However, in recent years opinion has moved away from the idea of packing everybody into a formal, rigid system of objectives. Today, when maximum flexibility is essential, achieving that rightly seems more important.

**"A manager's job should be based on a task to be performed in order to attain the company's objectives... the manager should be directed and controlled by the objectives of performance rather than by his boss."** *The Practice of Management*

PETER DRUCKER

# Achieving a balance

**F**lexibility has always had great importance for Drucker. As Micklethwait and Wooldridge argue, the fading of MBO has been linked with a rising "fashion for that other great Drucker theme, handing decisions back to workers through delayering and empowerment". They ask: "Why did the prophet of empowerment turn to such a rigid approach to management?" The answer is that he did not: other students of management theory did so, in their development of his ideas. But the two writers are correct to observe that Drucker "was trying – as he has done ever since – to create a balance between what was best in both the humanist and rationalist" schools of management.

That balance has to be struck, not by thinkers, but by practising managers. Turning their aims into successful actions, says Drucker, forces managers to master five basic operations: setting objectives, organizing the group, motivating and communicating, measuring performance, and developing people, including yourself (see p. 33). These MBO operations are all compatible with empowerment, if you truly follow Alfred P. Sloan's principle of decentralization: telling people what you want done, but letting them achieve it their own way. To make the principle work well, people need to be able to develop personally, which Drucker viewed as the most important part of the five operations.

In addition, for the quintet to succeed, you have to forget a fallacy that, according to Drucker, underlies almost everything ever written about people management: "There is one right way to manage people – or at least there should be". Drucker himself once believed in the fallacy but unusually, on this issue he radically changed his mind. In *The Practice of Management* he more or less accepted that

Douglas McGregor's "Theory Y", which maintains that the natural instinct of everyone is to work willingly and well, was the only sound approach to managing people. But eight years later Abraham Maslow proved Drucker "dead wrong", showing "conclusively that different people have to be managed differently" if they are to perform well and achieve their potential.

This is the antithesis of a rigid MBO system. Fascinatingly, there is not a single mention of "objectives" in the index to Drucker's 1999 book, *Management Challenges for the 21st Century*. The single aspect of his thought with which Drucker has been most identified no longer looms large – or indeed even looms at all. However, he does suggest a new starting point for management theory and practice that is not too far removed: a "definition of results" and then "managing for performance" to achieve those results.

## Managing for results

In 1964, a decade after publication of the definitive *The Practice of Management*, Drucker published a "how-to" book entitled *Managing for Results*. It expands the theory of MBO into the only place where meaningful results can be won: the outside world. The theory of how to "produce results on the outside, in the market and the economy" rests on eight perceptions, neatly summarized by Jack Beatty in *The World According to Drucker*:

- Resources and results exist outside, not inside, the business.
- Results come from exploiting opportunities, not solving problems.

- For results, resources must go to opportunities, not to problems.
- "Economic results" do not go to minor players in a given market, but to leaders.
- Leadership, however, is not likely to last.
- What exists is getting old.
- What exists is likely to be misallocated (i.e., the first 10 per cent of effort produces 90 per cent of the results).
- To achieve economic results, concentrate.

This list is plainly aimed at top management, and is concerned with strategy (a word Drucker used to spurn, but to which he has become reconciled). A solid, sound strategy is customer-focused, entrepreneurial, aimed at market leadership, based on innovation, and tightly focused on "decisive opportunities".

# Individual responsibility

The crucial argument for MBO was that it created a link between top management's strategic thinking and the strategy's implementation lower down. But the required nature of the link has changed profoundly since 1964.

The critical difference is that responsibility for objectives has been passed, as Drucker shows, from the organization to its individual members: "in the knowledge-based organization all members have to be able to control their own work by feeding back from their results to their objectives". Writing 40 years after *The Practice of Management*, Drucker says that this is what he called "Management by Objectives" and "Self Control" (see p. 61). The underlining is his. Today the worker is a self-manager, whose decisions are of decisive importance for results.

Drucker cites as a current example the mini-mill that makes steel with under 100 workers, one-tenth the number of a conventional plant with similar output. Each worker, he points out, "makes decisions all the time that have a greater impact on the results of the entire mini-mill than even middle managers ever had in the conventional mill". In such an organization, management has to ask each employee three questions:

■ What should we hold you accountable for?
■ What information do you need?
■ What information do you owe the rest of us?

Each worker, under this arrangement, participates in the key decisions on equipment, scheduling, and "indeed what the basic business policy of the entire mill should be". Drucker asserts that people managed in this way – people who know more about the job than anybody else – react to being held responsible by acting responsibly. This is an essential principle of "empowerment", the movement that gathered so much inspiration from Drucker's work. His commitment to the principle has never wavered, although he dislikes the term.

Empowerment recognizes "the demise" of the command-and-control system, but remains a term of power and rank. True, people are still subordinates in the sense that they can be "hired or fired, promoted, appraised, and so on". But the "superior" is increasingly dependent on the subordinates for getting results in their areas of responsibility, where they (and not the boss) have the requisite knowledge. "In turn these 'subordinates' depend on the superior for direction. They depend on the superior to tell them what the 'score' is."

**Conducting knowledge workers**
*A manager should view members of his or her team much as a conductor regards the players in the orchestra, as individuals whose particular skills contribute to the success of the enterprise.*

# The management orchestra

The word "score" is carefully chosen. Drucker's favourite metaphor for modern management is musical. In his opinion, the superior-subordinate relationship "is far more like that between the conductor of an orchestra and the instrumentalist" than the traditional organizational norm. "In the knowledge-based company, the superior cannot as a rule do the work of the supposed subordinate any more than the conductor... can play the tuba," states Drucker. However, everybody knows what piece the orchestra is playing, what results everybody wishes to achieve, and what specific part each of them has to play. All the members of the orchestra work together using the same score, as a band of skilled individualists.

There is nothing the conductor, however able or autocratic, can achieve without the willing support and contribution of the players. Increasingly, full-time employees have to be managed "as if they were volunteers". Because they receive no pay, volunteers tend to require greater job satisfaction than paid workers. Drucker thinks, however, that non-volunteer needs are just the same:

■ Challenge, above all
■ "To know the organization's mission and to believe in it"
■ Continuous training
■ The "need to see results"

Thus, the development of the knowledge society has finally brought about that elusive "balance between what was best in both the humanist and rationalist" schools of management. The organization and its senior management are as intently focused on results as ever. But the other people in the organization fulfil its needs and their own, not in response to top-down dictation, but by effectively exercising their own abilities and motivation.

**"... the knowledge worker is dependent on the superior to give direction and, above all, to define what the 'score' is for the entire organization, that is, what are standards and values, performance and results."** *Management Challenges for the 21st Century*

# Intelligent self-management

The issue of personal effectiveness has long occupied Drucker, whose 1966 book, *The Effective Executive*, reads like the individual's companion volume to the organization's *Managing for Results*. Drucker had been very impressed by his observations of "self-control" at General Electric. He liked the fact that GE's unit managers, and not their superiors, received the results of the annual audit. He believed that a GE atmosphere of "confidence and trust in the company" could be traced to "using information for self-control rather than control from above".

Self-control is the tool of effectiveness. Drucker distinguishes powerfully between "efficient" (doing something well) and "effective" (doing the right thing well). The effective executive knows what to do, knows how to do it, and (above all) gets it done. In all three phases, the effective executive exercises intelligent self-management, starting with the management of their own time. They use that time systematically for work that only they can do, and they establish priorities by putting first things first — and putting second things nowhere. They also take decisions effectively — or some of them do.

# Know yourself

Despite his belief in people and their potential, Drucker sometimes writes as if innate qualities cannot be altered. He poses as a "crucial question" for managers whether "I produce results as a decision-maker or an adviser", and adds: "The person who has learned that he or she is not a decision-maker should have learned to say 'No' when offered a decision-making assignment". The distinction is impractical, however, as managers at every

**Freedom to manage yourself**
*The laptop computer frees managers to work wherever and whenever they choose. It is the perfect tool for knowledge workers, who rely chiefly on themselves for motivation and direction.*

level have to take decisions whether they want to or not, for example, on people issues. Here Drucker offers useful advice, which any manager would be wise to follow. He suggests managers ask themselves the following four questions, regarding an employee:

- What has he or she done well?
- What is the person likely to do well?
- What do they have to learn to be able to get the full benefit from their strength?
- If I had a son or daughter, would I be willing to have them work under this person?

He has similarly thought through the process of decision-making in general, and gives equally shrewd advice about the practicalities. For example, he suggests separating the recurrent issues (which are handled by the system) from the unique (which are dealt with independently); and he advises on how to determine which decisions to delegate and which to retain. It is hard to think of any manager who would not benefit from learning to ask the right questions to obtain the right information. But when Drucker also insists that "people way down the line" have to "learn how to... make effective decisions", he again throws doubt on his distinction between the innate decision-maker and the innate adviser.

Drucker also believes that there are two distinctive ways of absorbing information − through the written or the spoken language − and that everyone tends to have a leaning towards being either a 'reader' or a 'listener'. He argues that knowing your style is the "first thing to know about how one performs", lamenting the fact that very few people indeed know "which of the two they are", even though this ignorance is "damaging". Once you understand which is your naturally dominant learning style you are in a position to improve the way you perform. Drucker advises: "... do not try to change yourself − it is unlikely to be successful. But work, and hard, to improve the way you perform. And try not to do work of any kind in a way you do not perform or perform badly."

This sage advice has to be squared with the statement that "more and more people in the workforce will have to manage themselves. They will have to place themselves where they can make the greatest contribution; they will have to develop themselves." Drucker believes that there are "many" areas where the individual lacks "the minimum endowment needed", so the energy, resources, and time should go, not into making "an incompetent person into a low mediocrity", but into making "a competent person into a star performer".

# Know where you belong

Drucker stresses that "how a person performs" is just as much a "given" as their strengths and weaknesses. "A few common personality traits" (such as the difference between readers and listeners) "usually determine how one achieves results". You plan your objectives, therefore, to fit the givens, but "to be able to manage oneself", you finally have to know the answer to the question: "What are my values?" The answer indicates what organization you should join: its values and your own must be "close enough so that they can coexist".

When you know your strengths of ability and performance and your values, you can find where you "belong". Then the self-manager must ask not the MBO question "What am I told to contribute?" but the post-MBO question "What should I contribute?" Drucker regards this as "a new question in human history" because "until very recently, it was taken for granted that most people were subordinates who did as they were told". This is generally still the case, so Drucker is being somewhat Utopian in his latest formula for effectiveness, in which the manager asks him or herself:

■ What does the situation require?
■ How could I make my greatest contribution with my strengths, my way of performing, my values, to what needs to be done?
■ What results have to be achieved to make a difference?

This leads to action conclusions: what to do, where to start, how to start, what goals and deadlines to set. The formula differs hardly at all from the definition of effectiveness Drucker has always used: knowing what to do and how to do it, and getting it done. The difference lies, however, in transferring all the responsibility to the individual, not to "do one's own thing", but to set and achieve one's own objectives – one's unique contribution.

## Ideas into action

■ Understand that there is no one right way to manage people.

■ For best results, give resources to opportunities, not to problems.

■ Get to know the organization's mission and to believe in it.

■ Find out what you should do, and how – then go ahead and do it.

■ Ask yourself whether you produce results as a decision-maker or an adviser.

■ Help yourself and others to learn how to manage yourselves.

■ Ask yourself what you should do, rather than simply doing what you are told to do.

# Managing by objectives

*he essential message taught by Drucker through Management by Objectives is that managers need to identify and set objectives both for themselves, their units, and their organizations. Ensure that you set the right objectives if you want to achieve the right results.*

### What is MBO?

The principle behind MBO is to make sure that everybody within the organization has a clear understanding of the aims, or objectives, of that organization, as well as an awareness of their own roles and responsibilities in achieving those aims.

### MBO and the individual

Start with yourself by reading the following six questions and answering them as best you can. The responsibility on all six counts rests with you as an individual. None of the answers depends entirely on other people, and some do not depend on them at all.

PETER DRUCKER

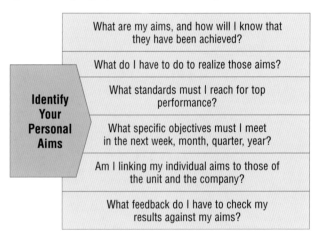

| Identify Your Personal Aims | What are my aims, and how will I know that they have been achieved? |
| | What do I have to do to realize those aims? |
| | What standards must I reach for top performance? |
| | What specific objectives must I meet in the next week, month, quarter, year? |
| | Am I linking my individual aims to those of the unit and the company? |
| | What feedback do I have to check my results against my aims? |

If you can answer some of the questions only partially, try to find out what you need to know in order to answer them fully. Keep returning to your answers to check that you are still working along the right lines, and review them as necessary – you will find that many of your answers change over time.

## MBO and the organization

There are too many managers who think and act as if the higher strategy of their organization is no business of theirs – in fact, it is everybody's vital business. Never forget that your organization's objectives affect you directly and personally. Refer back to the questions on the opposite page – it only takes small changes in the wording of the questions to make them apply to your company and to your unit. Repeat the exercise, writing down the answers, first as if you are the boss of your unit (whatever your actual position), and then as if you are the chief executive. If you do not know some of the answers, try to obtain them.

## Personal empowerment

If you find that you cannot identify your or your company's aims satisfactorily, remember what Drucker advocates: you need four powers to do an excellent job. These four powers are a combination of the personal qualities that an individual brings to the job, and the powers made available to everyone by the organization. The powers are not only essential to perform an excellent job, but also to produce job satisfaction, the prime motivator.

| The Four Powers |
| :---: |
| **1** Freedom to challenge everything and anything |
| **2** Continuous training and development on the job |
| **3** Knowledge of, and faith in, the organization's mission |
| **4** The ability to achieve and see results |

## The right organization

If your company or unit does not have an overall objective that you can identify, or you are unable to challenge their strategy, your ability to grow on the job will be hamstrung, and your efforts to achieve real results will become frustrated. Some organizations may place a lower priority than you might like on allowing staff to exercise the four powers. In either case, find somewhere else where you can really make a contribution – and go there!

# 1 Making a contribution

Be aware of what is expected of you and why – this is one of the most valuable lessons of Drucker's teachings. That awareness will determine your ability to contribute to your organization.

## Asking the right questions

The question "What is MY contribution?" needs to be properly understood within the context of the organization. Which of the following three questions is the most apt?

■ What do I WANT to contribute?
■ What am I TOLD to contribute?
■ What SHOULD I contribute?

The last question is the most appropriate one to ask. It means "What does the situation require?" Once you have succeeded in identifying what is required, you can start to consider how you can use your own unique powers to contribute to what needs to be done.

| Your Unique Powers | | |
|---|---|---|
| Your strengths | Your way of performing | Your values |

## Identifying strengths

To understand how you can best match your unique powers to your required contribution, carry out a SWOT analysis on yourself. Draw a box with four compartments. Set down your Strengths in one, your Weaknesses in another, then list your Opportunities and the Threats to your success in the third and fourth compartments. The required contribution should rely on your strengths and not depend on areas in which you are weak. It should give you opportunities to shine, but should not involve threats to your personal fulfilment. Ask:

■ Will my contribution involve doing what I really want to do?
■ Will it be rewarding and stimulating?

If you would really rather be doing something else, and if the rewards and interest you need are lacking, it is foolish to continue. Your contribution will inevitably fall short in the area that should dominate everything: results. Drucker's advice is paramount. Always ask: "Where and how can I have results that make a difference?"

PETER DRUCKER

# 2 Setting standards

The temptation for all managers is to find something at which they excel, and which comes quite easily, and to continue doing it for as long as possible. If you want to improve as a manager, however, adapt your contribution to change, and see each level of achievement as a stepping stone to something higher and better.

## Improving performance

In searching to identify where your results can really make a difference, follow these guidelines:

- Choose target results that "stretch" your abilities above and beyond your present limits.
- Pick a target that is achievable, but at the same time one which enlarges the bounds of possibility.
- Make sure the results will be meaningful and clearly visible.
- Unless it is absolutely impossible (which is rarely the case), find a way of measuring your results.

Never be satisfied by present standards of performance, whether other people's or your own. If you can find superior performance elsewhere, in your own company or outside, make bettering that level your benchmark. Make a personal habit, too, of selecting key aspects of your work which you can measurably improve, such as answering your phone within five rings or arriving at meetings five minutes early, and ask colleagues to help keep you up to scratch.

### Exceeding Targets

What actually is achievable can exceed your wildest dreams, as illustrated by the following case study. You should never set your staff unachievable targets – it is a pointless exercise and will be demoralizing for them.

James Adamson saved NCR's factory in Dundee from extinction by turning it into the world's prime source of automatic teller machines (ATMs) for banks. Yet Dundee started from far behind the leaders in the field – ninth in the world. NCR's first two ATMs, moreover, were so terrible that the customers returned them. Adamson called in his engineers and asked them not just to match competitors' reliability, but to do twice as well. He was laughed at, but he refused to give up – and the engineers found out how to improve reliability, not twice, but threefold.

# 3 Making it happen

"What 'impossible' things can I accomplish?" Base your answer on three key elements: your individual talent, having a true "stretch target", and achieving your chosen contribution. You will achieve this last, all-important element if you are successful in execution.

## What, how, where, and when?

Drucker breaks down execution into making four decisions. Make it your practice to plan systematically, never failing to address these four decisions, and always work to a realistic deadline.

| The Four Decisions of Execution | | | |
|---|---|---|---|
| **1** What to do | **2** How to start | **3** Where to start | **4** What goals and deadlines to set |

James Adamson's thinking at Dundee (see p. 69) is an excellent example of four-stage execution. The "What" was to improve reliability. The starting point was re-engineering the product. The "Where" was in the engineering department. The goal was doubled reliability – and he set a deadline for its achievement. The director of engineering went through exactly the same process in going beyond his boss's request to achieve the "impossible". In addition to exceeding the goal originally set by Adamson, an invaluable consequence of this success was to improve the overall efficiency and effectiveness of the whole operation.

| Unlocking the Key |
|---|
| Successful achievement of an objective may depend on finding the "key" to a specific aspect of the operation. Learn from a case study cited by Drucker in which the "key" unlocked the full potential of a stagnating enterprise. |

A hospital administrator needed to revitalize a large hospital, and found the "unlocking key" in the emergency room, which was "big, visible, and sloppy". What to do? How to start? Where to start? The administrator gave the ER staff an extremely stretching target: every patient had to be seen by a qualified nurse within one minute of arrival. The deadline for achievement was two years. In the event, the target was met in half that time. Two years later, the whole hospital had been transformed.

PETER DRUCKER

# Managing yourself

The skills, qualities, and values you bring to your job are of crucial importance in achieving your objectives. Aim to be the kind of manager who gets the best from staff, and who does the best for them.

## Assessing yourself

Drucker's advice on hiring people can be turned inside out to provide a searching test of how good a manager you are. Drucker tells recruiters to look for evidence of past success, potential for further achievement, the ability to learn more, and the qualities of a good manager. Assess yourself on these four points to identify areas in which you should improve. Analyze your answers very carefully, making sure that they are totally honest.

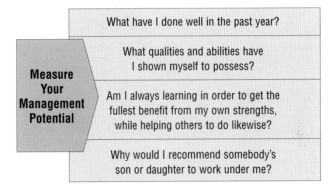

**Measure Your Management Potential**

What have I done well in the past year?

What qualities and abilities have I shown myself to possess?

Am I always learning in order to get the fullest benefit from my own strengths, while helping others to do likewise?

Why would I recommend somebody's son or daughter to work under me?

## Consider your values

Drucker is insistent that playing your part, which he refers to as "managing oneself", depends on your values as well as on your strengths, weaknesses, and personality. One of the essential values is honesty. If you are honest with yourself, you will treat other people honestly too. Never work in an organization whose values are unacceptable to you. Ignore this principle and you will condemn yourself to frustration and non-performance. "In respect to ethics", writes Drucker, "the rules are the same for everybody." There is only one test – "the mirror test" – and you must make sure you pass it. It consists of one question: "What kind of person do I want to see when I shave myself, or put on my lipstick, in the morning?"

# 4

# Harnessing the power of innovation

How to seek out, respond to, and exploit change as opportunity ● **Watching out for significant changes in population, perception, and knowledge** ● Why bright ideas are important, but purposeful innovation matters more ● **Mastering the five do's and the three don'ts of successful innovation** ● Why entrepreneurs seek to define and confine risks ● **Keeping new ventures well apart from the company's established business** ● Using the "business X-ray" to discover how much innovation you need

**D**rucker calls innovation "the specific tool of entrepreneurs". Doing new things, or doing old things in new ways, is how entrepreneurs "exploit change as an opportunity for a different business or a different service". They "see change as the norm and as healthy". Usually they do not bring about the change themselves. But... "the entrepreneur always searches for change, responds to it, and exploits it as an opportunity".

This process of exploitation, Drucker says, had a profound influence on the American economy as the 20th century approached its end. In the period between 1974 and 1984, the total number of jobs in the US economy grew by a record 24 per cent, while Western Europe's job losses totalled between three and four million. Nor was the American growth solely, or even mainly, high-tech. Although the high-tech explosion was special, "of immeasurable qualitative importance", the new jobs came "from anywhere and nowhere" as "new applications of management" made possible "the emergence of the entrepreneurial economy".

These observations inspired Drucker to write *Innovation and Entrepreneurship* (1984), which was then, and remains, the best manual on the practice and principles of its subject. As with management 30 years before, Drucker tackled innovation as a discipline that can be taught and learnt, the sources, nature, and symptoms of which can all be studied. By studying innovation, the entrepreneur and the entrepreneurial manager learn where and how to succeed. Turning innovative ideas into profitable action is the essence of the entrepreneur. Typically, Drucker tore away the mystique surrounding his theme. "Entrepreneurship is risky", he snorted, "mainly because so few of the so-called entrepreneurs know what they are doing."

# Searching for changes

The book set out to remedy that defect. Drucker is convinced that innovation can be approached methodically, by a "purposeful and organized search for changes" and by identifying the opportunities that such changes might offer. Within the established company or industry, he isolated four sources for these entrepreneurial opportunities:

- The unexpected – the unexpected success, the unexpected failure, the unexpected outside event.
- The incongruity – between reality as it actually is and reality as it is assumed to be or as it "ought to be".
- Innovation based on process need.
- Changes in industry structure or market structure that catch everyone unawares.

As always, Drucker has vivid, wide-ranging examples to support each source of entrepreneurial opportunitiy. For the unexpected success, he cites the unexpected demand for TVs from "poor" Japanese farmers, which was exploited by Matsushita, but by nobody else. For the unexpected failure, he gives the example of the surprise flop of the Edsel, a large, "gas-guzzling" sedan, which opened Ford's eyes to fundamental market changes. The company then exploited this change with the launch of the sporty, smaller Thunderbird. In his discussion of incongruities, Drucker cites the rise of the mini-mill at the expense of large integrated steel mills, and loading containers on land instead of loading freighters on the water. To illustrate process need, he quotes an innovation in eye surgery, while structural change brings mention of the shift in US physicians from single to group practice.

# External sources of changes

This quartet of sources visible within the enterprise or its industry are only part of the story. Drucker also identifies three external sources:

- Demographics (population changes)
- Changes in perception, mood and meaning
- New knowledge, both scientific and non-scientific

Dead certainty can always be found in the first of these sources. One example of demographic certainty is a "forecast" that Drucker made in 1957. By combining the increase in births (which had already happened) with another established trend, the rise in the proportion of young adults going to college, Drucker estimated that there would be 10 to 12 million students by the 1970s – a huge increase. Nearly all the large US universities regarded this as preposterous but the new entrepreneurial universities exploited this dead-cert prediction to their great profit.

As an example of a change in perception, Drucker mentions the spread of "dining", as opposed to merely "eating", from the well-to-do to the less privileged. As for new knowledge, innovators who want to exploit it, he stresses, need only apply "a careful analysis of the knowledge available and the knowledge needed". He cites his own success in the field of management as an example:

**"Entrepreneurs need to search purposefully for the sources of innovation, the changes and their symptoms that indicate opportunities for successful innovation."** *Innovation & Entrepreneurship*

PETER DRUCKER

"Many of the required pieces of knowledge were already available: organization theory, for instance, but also quite a bit of knowledge about managing work and worker. My analysis also showed, however, that these pieces were scattered and lodged in half a dozen different disciplines. Then it found which key knowledges were missing: purpose of a business; and knowledge of the work and structure of top management; what we now term 'business policy' and 'strategy'; objectives; and so on."

His response was to provide the missing pieces and combine them with the others to form a coherent whole.

# Innovative bright ideas

**D**espite this personal example, the classification of sources does not altogether work. It is too schematic. As Drucker himself admits, these "seven source areas of innovative opportunities are blurred, and there is considerable overlap between them". Innovation cannot be tied down as easily as Drucker suggests — which in effect he admits when he says that "innovations based on a bright idea probably outnumber all other categories put together".

The untidiness of bright ideas bothers him. They are the "riskiest and least successful" source, and no one knows which ideas "have a chance to succeed and which ones are likely to fail". Attempts have been made to reduce this unpredictability, but have not been "particularly successful". Bright ideas are also "vague and elusive". For all that, Drucker states that "an entrepreneurial economy cannot dismiss cavalierly the innovation based on a bright idea". He cannot escape from the fact that the genesis and fate of innovation, ultimately, follow no rules.

# Principles of innovation

**D**rucker still sticks to his schematic guns: "The purposeful innovation resulting from analysis, system, and hard work... surely covers at least 90 per cent of all effective innovations." It is unlike Drucker to put forward a statistic with no hard supporting evidence. He is on firmer ground when arguing that general principles do exist, which he labels "do's", "don'ts", and "conditions". The "do's" are:

- Analyze the opportunities.
- Go out to look, to ask, to listen.
- Keep it simple, keep it focused.
- Start small – try to do one specific thing.
- Aim at market leadership.

The fifth principle – thinking big – seems to contrast illogically with the fourth. But, as Drucker says, "Innovations had better be capable of being started small, requiring at first little money, few people, and only a small and limited market." That gives the innovator more time (and space) within which to correct the inevitable errors. All the time, however, you "aim at dominance in an industry or market". Don't undershoot, or you "will simply create an opportunity for the competition" – which could be taken as another "don't" to add to the following list:

- Don't try to be clever.
- Don't diversify, don't splinter, don't try to do too many things at once.
- Don't try to innovate for the future.

The first and last "don'ts" are counter-intuitive but their sense quickly becomes apparent. "Innovations have to be handled by ordinary human beings [whose] incompetence is…in abundant and never-failing supply. Anything too clever is almost bound to fail." As for the future, Drucker advises "innovate for the present!" in the sense that the innovation, if it could be successful this instant, will be just as successful in the future. It may take ten years of development to bring a new drug to market, but the medical condition that it will cure is prevalent right now.

These pragmatic recommendations are hardly consistent with the romantic image of risk-taking entrepreneurs. But Drucker dismisses this icon. He observes that entrepreneurs mostly cut "unromantic figures, and are much more likely

**Master of innovation**
*An inventive genius, who took out more than 1,000 patents, Thomas Alva Edison (1847–1931) found it impossible to manage any of the companies he formed once they reached medium size.*

to spend hours on a cashflow projection than to dash off looking for 'risks'". Most innovators, in his experience, "are successful to the extent to which they define risks and confine them". What governs their success is the way in which they "systematically analyze the sources of innovative opportunity, then pinpoint the opportunity and exploit it". They are conservative people, focused not on risk, but on opportunity.

# Managing innovation separately

Unlike most writers on entrepreneurship, Drucker goes beyond this point to the crucial matter of management. How does entrepreneurial management differ from the usual variety? Both have to be "systematic, organized, purposeful". But if an entrepreneurial business is placed inside an established management system, it is more than likely to fail.

Drucker maintains that the established company will load insupportable burdens on the new venture: burdensome examples include highly structured reward schemes, return-on-investment targets, and lack of clear accountability for the venture. So should companies abandon all efforts to govern new ventures? What about the policies and practices which Drucker recommends? He himelf asks: "Don't they interfere with the entrepreneurial spirit and stifle creativity? Cannot a business be entrepreneurial without such policies and practices?" His answer is that you might get away with it, but "neither very successfully, nor for very long".

Drucker is deeply aware of the fundamental difficulty in converting a large organization, which has built up policies, people, and practices along set lines, into the anarchic modes of the entrepreneur. He is full of warnings: "the most important caveat is not to mix managerial units and entrepreneurial ones" in any way. Also, steer clear of diversification, which, whatever its other benefits, "does not mix with entrepreneurship and innovation". Finally, don't try to solve the problem by "buying in" – acquiring small entrepreneurial ventures. He observes that "I myself know of no case where 'buying in' has worked."

# Forming the business X-ray

Not only must the "entrepreneurial, the new" be organized completely separately from "the old and existing", but "there has to be a special locus for the new venture within the organization, and it has to be pretty high up". However small the new venture may be in relation to its parent, "somebody in top management must have the specific assignment to work on tomorrow as an entrepreneur and innovator".

Among other needs, this manager is responsible for "the business X-ray", which "furnishes the information needed to define how much innovation a given business requires, in what areas, and within what time frame". To discover this information Drucker suggests asking four questions, which are based on the work of management consultant Michael J. Kami. They are:

- How much longer will this product still grow?
- How much longer will it maintain itself in the marketplace?
- How soon can it be expected to age and decline – and how fast?
- When will it become obsolescent?

The answers establish the gap between what already exists and what is required to achieve the corporate ambitions: "the gap has to be filled or the company will soon start to die". But Drucker maintains that the company needs to aim beyond the measured gap because of the high probability of failure and (even higher) delay. "A company therefore should have under way at least three times the innovative efforts which, if successful, would fill the gap." In Drucker's experience, most executives find this threefold demand too high. In fact, the logic is irrefutable.

# Managing new ventures

The issues of managing an entrepreneurial venture are at least as acute outside established businesses, in brand-new operations. Drucker puts it neatly: "In the existing business, it is the existing that is the main obstacle to entrepreneurship." In the new venture, it is its absence. Every one of the great Thomas Edison's companies "collapsed ignominiously once it got to middle size, and was saved only by booting Edison himself out and replacing him with professional management". Wonderful as an inventor, Edison never mastered all four requirements for managing the development of a new venture:

- A focus on the market.
- Financial foresight, especially in planning for cashflow and capital needs ahead.
- Building a top management team long before the new venture actually needs one and long before it can actually afford one.
- A decision by the founding entrepreneur in respect of his or her own role, area of work, and relationships.

An example would be the foundation of Compaq Computer, whose successful attack on the portable computer market was based on this quartet of principles. But none of these four requirements is cut and dried. "When a new venture does succeed, more often than not it is in a market other than the one it was originally intended to serve, with products or services not quite those with which it had set out, bought in large part by customers it did not even think of when it started, and used for a host of purposes besides the ones for which the products were first designed." "Market focus" in these circumstances means flexibility: spotting what has gone wrong, and moving quickly to turn error into advantage.

Financial focus, too, requires entrepreneurs to change their minds: "Entrepreneurs starting new ventures... tend to be greedy. They therefore focus on profits. But this is the wrong focus for a new venture, or rather, it comes last rather than first." Cashflow, capital, and controls come much earlier in the new venture's development. Without them "the profit figures are fiction – good for 12 or 18 months, after which they evaporate". Drucker stresses that financial foresight demands more thought than time.

Even if the new enterprise gets its market focus and financial foresight right, "serious crisis" threatens unless a common ailment, "lack of top management", is cured. Drucker pinpoints the catch-22 difficulty. If you cannot afford top management, how can you obtain it? His answer is to build the team from within, by dividing roles among the founding group and developing their management skills. All this, however, is plainly easier said than done, partly because the founder or founders have to evolve – and to devolve authority. Few find it easy either to articulate their proper role or to step back (let alone step down).

# Entrepreneurial strategies

Forming strategy comes much easier than forming management structure, in the sense that every entrepreneur has some kind of plan. Drucker has isolated four strategies that he thinks specifically entrepreneurial:

- Being "Fustest with the Mostest" – the "greatest gamble", aiming from the beginning at permanent leadership
- "Hitting Them Where They Ain't" – either by "creative imitation", which surpasses the original innovation; or by "entrepreneurial judo", a concept highly developed by the Japanese, which enables newcomers "to catapult themselves into a leadership position... against the entrenched, established companies".
- Finding and occupying a specialized "ecological niche" – "obtaining a practical monopoly in a small area".
- Changing the economic characteristics of a product, a market, or an industry – by "creating utility", or pricing, or adaptation to the customer's social and economic reality, or delivering what represents true value to the customer.

He gives examples for each method of achieving the fourth strategy. For utility he cites Rowland Hill's penny post; for pricing he cites Gillette's cheap razors with dear blades; for adaptation to the customer's reality, he provides the example of Cyrus McCormick's leasing of harvesters to farmers; and for delivering true value, he cites Herman Miller's move from selling individual items of furniture to offering whole office systems. Drucker recognizes the difficulty of all this diversity: "it is far less easy to be specific about entrepreneurial strategies than it is about purposeful innovation and entrepreneurial management".

He nevertheless makes a formidable effort to systematize an activity that makes up its own rules as it goes along. Inevitably the effort falls short of the aim. But there's not one innovator or entrepreneur who cannot benefit from Drucker's analytical approach – and that goes doubly, if not trebly, for managers.

## Ideas into action

- Maintain a purposeful and organized search for new opportunities.

- Look for incongruity between reality and what it is assumed to be or "ought" to be.

- Innovate for a present need, not for a future possibility.

- Give a new venture a high-up godfather or godmother to whom it reports.

- Keep flexible – spot what goes wrong and turn error to advantage.

- Focus on cashflow, capital, and controls – not profit.

- Build your team from within, developing its own management skills.

# Recognizing the sea-change

Drucker's emergence as a profound thinker on society, the economy, and politics predates his discovery of management. His thinking was years ahead of his time, although founded on close observation of the present.

His first two books, *The End of Economic Man* (1939) and *The Future of Industrial Man* (1942) established him as an insightful political scientist. *The Age of Discontinuity*, published in 1969, was decades in advance of conventional thinking – and his predictions were proved right.

Drucker spotted three discontinuities: in technology and industry, the world economy, and government. Of the three, it was the first that proved crucial. He saw four techno-industrial changes, including new materials, exploitation of the oceans, home working, and the rise of the information industry. The first three visions all had substance; only the fourth was an inspired reading of the present, and thus of the future.

In a later book, Drucker expressed his discovery in suitably apocalyptic terms: "With the advent of the computer, information became the organizing principle of production. With this a new basic civilization came into being." Writing 13 years

before the IBM PC changed the world of computing, and 24 years before the World Wide Web opened for business, in *The Age of Discontinuity* Drucker compared the future abundance of information with electricity.

## Knowledge workers

He saw that the determining power in the economy and in society would be knowledge, which he defined as "systematic, purposeful, organized knowledge". A new army of "knowledge workers" was coming to the fore, and its soldiers would impose new norms on organizations and society as a whole.

They would be first among the millions of home workers; they would be the leaders in rewriting the rules of employment – by changing employers and careers more readily. They would be a major force in creating new demands for goods and services as the world moved from an international economy to a world economy. *The Age of Discontinuity* set the intellectual

PETER DRUCKER

> **"Certainly young people, a few years hence, will use information systems as their normal tools, much as they now use the typewriters and the telephone."** *The World According to Peter Drucker* by Jack Beatty

agenda for the upheavals that were to come – which Drucker continued to monitor and explain with uncanny precision. Books like *The New Realities* (1989), *Managing for the Future* (1992), and *Post-Capitalist Society* (1993) described a society that could not have been predicted by extrapolation from the past.

Drucker forced recognition that the discontinuities changed everything. "A great deal these days", he wrote, "is being said about the impact of the new information technologies on material civilization, on goods, services, and businesses. The social impacts are however as important – they may be more important." One was an entre-preneurial surge: Drucker saw innovations in politics, govern-ment, education, economics, the national state, the city.

*The Age of Discontinuity* did not create this sea-change. But it marked out the new sea-scape, named its features, and irre-versibly changed perceptions to take account of the new realities.

# 5

# Responsible knowledge management

Making the service economy and knowledge workers more productive ● **Predicting the future by fully understanding the present** ● Why knowledge continually makes itself obsolete ● **The need to shift from inside information to external information** ● Employing people as outside contractors rather than internal staff ● **How the non-profit organizations can teach management lessons to businesses** ● The emergence of knowledge as the "absolutely decisive factor of production"

**H**ow does the manager exploit the great trends in society and the economy? Broad historical changes have been Drucker's dominant themes from the beginning of his writing career. He was the first to define the "great divide" of the 20th century, a seismic split that produced and is producing major social change: the knowledge revolution. As manual work has become fabulously more productive, thanks in recent decades partly to the new technology of information, the manual labour force has become a minority – following in the footsteps of farm workers. According to Drucker, the challenge for management today is to make the service economy and knowledge workers (see p. 93) far more productive, again using the new electronic armoury.

Since the 1980s, if not earlier, Drucker has been looking beyond the millennium. Yet he disclaims any intention of posing as a prophet. In 1986, he characteristically argued that the millennium was already here, that "we are well advanced" past that landmark, and emphasized that he had never written about the "next century". He has now. In 1999 he published *Management Challenges for the 21st Century*. It represents a typical balance between Drucker's views of eternal verities and his acute analysis of changing forces in management.

**"For the next twenty or thirty years demographics will dominate the politics of all developed countries. And they will inevitably be politics of *great turbulence*. No country is prepared for the issues."** *Management Challenges for the 21st Century*

# Identifying future developments

An especially cogent statement of Drucker's overall vision was published considerably earlier, in the September/October 1997 edition of the *Harvard Business Review*, which marked the 75th anniversary of the journal. Drucker has long been one of its most distinguished contributors. With typical assurance, he called the piece "The Future that has Already Happened". Predicting the future at all, let alone for the next 75 years, is pointless, he asserted. "But it is possible – and fruitful – to identify major events that have already happened, irrevocably, and that will have predictable effects in the next decade or two."

Drucker singled out demography as the first of these ineluctable forces. "The developed world is in the process of committing collective suicide. Its citizens are not having enough babies to reproduce themselves." Although you can definitely dispute his explanation (that younger people are cutting down on babies to offset the cost of looking after the aged), you cannot argue with the first two conclusions he draws from this depopulation of the West and of Japan (where a 56 per cent fall is predicted for the 21st century).

■ Retirement age will rise (Drucker expects this to be 75 well before 2010).

■ Economic growth can come only from a very sharp and continuing increase in the productivity of knowledge work and knowledge workers.

Drucker's third conclusion that "there will be no single dominant world economic power" is more difficult to agree with. Given the US domination of the new technologies it hardly convinces – especially as the US population is stable while other populations in the developed world are falling.

# Raising knowledge productivity

The overriding concern for Drucker is that all the developed countries, including the US, have a critical need for "continual systematic work on the productivity of knowledge and knowledge workers, which is abysmally low". Raising that productivity is the way to convert the developed world's quantitative lead in sheer numbers of knowledge workers into a qualitative one. Only thus will these states be enabled "to maintain their competitive position in the world economy". Knowledge productivity will not be the only competitive factor, but it is "likely to become decisive", at least for most industries in the developed countries.

Knowledge differs from all other resources in that it "constantly makes itself obsolete, with the result that today's advanced knowledge is tomorrow's ignorance". Drucker goes on to observe that "the knowledge that matters is subject to repeated and abrupt shifts", giving as examples the sudden impacts of pharmacology and applied genetics in health care, PCs and the Internet in computing. In fact, all four technologies have continued to develop — and, indeed, to interact. What Drucker is really saying is that new, disruptive technologies have been appearing at shorter and shorter intervals.

This phenomenon supports his "overarching" view "that the world economy will continue to be highly turbulent and highly competitive, prone to abrupt shifts". It is hard to imagine anybody, even someone far less perceptive than Drucker, believing otherwise. In this fast-moving and ever-shifting context, the information needs of business are also changing. Drucker writes with apparent approval of practices such as "activity-based costing", the "balanced scorecard", and "economic value analysis". But even these

PETER DRUCKER

innovations fall short in the drive to increase productivity because they aim only "at providing better information about events inside the company".

According to Drucker, "approximately 90 per cent or more of the information any organization collects is about inside events". The phrase "approximately 90 per cent or more" is one that, if uttered by a student, Drucker would certainly have shot down in flames for lack of precision and hard evidence – but it makes his point. His assertion is that "increasingly, a winning strategy will require information about events and conditions outside the institution: non-customers, technologies other than those that are currently used by the company and present competitors, markets not currently served, and so on."

# Managing knowledge workers

Developing rigorous methods for "garnering and analyzing outside information" is a "major challenge". Even if a business rises to the challenge, the revolutionary impact of the shift to the knowledge economy will remain inescapable. Knowledge workers, differing from their manual equivalents, "carry their knowledge in their heads, and therefore can take it with them". You cannot manage such people in the traditional manner. "In many cases they will not even be employees of the organization for which they work." Instead, contractors, experts, consultants, part-timers, joint-venture partners, and so on "will identify themselves by their own knowledge rather than by the organizations that pay them".

The whole meaning of organization, Drucker concludes, must change in consequence. He talks about the age-old search for the one "right" organization, up to and including "the present infatuation with teams". He states bluntly that "there can no longer be any such thing" as the one "right" organization. There never was, of course. Drucker has set up an Aunt Sally, which he conclusively knocks down. "Every organization in the developed countries (and not only businesses) will have to be designed for a specific task, time, and place (or culture)," he asserts.

## Extending the manager's role

In putting forward this argument Drucker is setting the stage for his *Harvard Business Review* peroration. "Management will increasingly extend beyond business enterprises, where it originated…as an attempt to organize the production of things". Now the emphasis has switched to the management of society's knowledge resources – "specifically, education and health care, both of which are today over-administered and undermanaged".

Two long-running Drucker themes flow together in his wide-ranging article. First, management's importance as a social institution is not synonymous with its economic importance. Management outside the business corporation – in non-profit-making organizations and in social institutions – is equally important in establishing the manager's claim to legitimacy and power. Second, the task facing management cannot be described in economic terms alone. Knowledge is not the exclusive property of the business class but a universal possession, the uses of which extend to all of society.

Behind Drucker's beliefs in the far-reaching role of management in society lies a third assumption, which is: what is, will be. Drucker ends the *Harvard Business Review* article by saying: "Predictions? Not at all. Those are solely

**Stock market "shareholder value"**
*Amid a climate of economic greed, in which shareholders acquire large profits, Drucker champions the non-profit-making sector and calls for a more responsible, longer-term perspective.*

the reasonable implications for a future that has already happened." But if education and health care are over-administered and undermanaged (as he rightly says) that statement cannot be true: their reform has hardly begun to take place. At bottom, Drucker is not simply a recording angel. He would otherwise have been a less potent and influential thinker. He has positive views about the directions society should take. So his hopes and wishes become "reasonable implications".

# Moral responsibility

PETER DRUCKER

**A** strong sense of moral purpose is one of the characteristics that sets Drucker apart from and above other writers on management. Even though he is recognized as the prophet of privatization (*The Age of Discontinuity*, 1969), Drucker has always had strictly limited faith in the powers of free enterprise, which in his opinion is only as good as its contribution to society. As the second half of the century – and his own thought – evolved, Drucker's definition of the society served by managers turned into a powerful critique. He argued in 1989 that society was "post-capitalist", "post-business", that even "in business proper, the values of business are no longer held with conviction and commitment".

That was plainly true of Drucker's own feelings. But since those words were written "business proper" has been indulging itself in some highly improper ways – and to Drucker's disapproval. At a time when the greatest stock-market boom in history was still creating and expanding gigantic fortunes, Drucker mentally turned his back on the profit-making sector. In May 1999 he told *The Observer*'s Simon Caulkin "I don't pretend to understand the current US economy". He pronounced himself "appalled and rather scared by the greed of today's executives".

Drucker cited as "both obscene and socially destructive" awards of $20 million bonuses "for firing 100,000 workers". Nor did he accept that management wonders justified the huge wealth currently being awarded to corporate executives. "I am not impressed by the way many businesses... are being managed," he stated. Where other commentators saw the end-century outpouring of Western riches as the beginning of a new growth economy, Drucker seemed to see the phenomenon as an ending. To quote

Caulkin, he thinks that "non-profit organizations – particularly in education, health, and religion – are the growth sector of the 21st century".

This emphasis on "non-profits" has featured in Drucker's writings for some time. He has a personal interest in some non-profits, as participant and adviser, and feels that, not only can they benefit from better management, but that they can teach its principles to commercial organizations. As so often, Drucker is turning the conventional management wisdom on its head.

# Corporate governance

Led by Thatcherite Britain, the theory and practice of the public sector have been dominated by the view that private-sector, profit-minded management would automatically yield far better results. But Drucker has no truck with the self-serving mysticism that surrounds the prevailing cult of "shareholder value", which tells boards of directors to maximize the share price (used to justify enormous rewards for those same directors). He regards "shareholder value" as entirely preoccupied with short-term results and calls for a balance between these and "the long-range prosperity and survival of the enterprise".

So what happens if directors show no interest in achieving this balance? That raises the whole issue of "corporate governance", already the subject of much debate. Drucker thinks the debate has only scratched the surface of what is going to be a major issue. He points out that knowledge workers, using their intellects as the tools of their trade, have opposed interests: as employees, shareholders, and future pensioners. The tensions aroused by these conflicts, he says, will have to be resolved.

Who will resolve the tensions? It cannot be "capitalists", according to Drucker, who argued in 1992 that they had been replaced by professional managers. "Instead of the old-line capitalist", moreover, "in developed countries pension funds increasingly control the supply and allocation of money." These funds in 1992 owned half the share capital of large US corporations and almost as much of their debt. "The beneficiary owners" are "the country's employees". Just as Karl Marx wanted, the employees own the means of production. Paradoxically, "the United States has become the most 'socialist' country around, while still being the most 'capitalist' one."

# Towards the knowledge society

PETER DRUCKER

**D**rucker asserts that "the real and controlling resource and the absolutely decisive 'factor of production' is now neither capital, nor land, nor labour. It is knowledge." He states in *Managing for the Future* (1992): "From now on the key is knowledge. The world is becoming not labour intensive, not materials intensive, not energy intensive, but knowledge intensive." A "new and very different" form of society is in consequence rapidly superseding capitalism. "The same forces" that destroyed Marxism and Communism are also "making capitalism obsolescent". The new post-capitalist society "will use the free market as the one proven source of economic integration". But the period is really one of "transition" to the "knowledge society" that "some of us dare hope for". This society is one that is built around the exchange of knowledge, and away from physical production and rampant capitalism.

Drucker saw this transition period as "a time to *make the future* – precisely because everything is in flux. This is a time for action." Despite this clarion call (addressed to everybody, right down to individuals), Drucker does not offer a plan of action. He instead issues directives. Pension funds, for example, *"have to make sure that the business is being managed"* (presumably, well-managed). He predicts, rather than prescribes, the "business audit", which will track "the performance of a company and of its management against a strategic plan and against specific objectives". Whether this will happen before his predicted time-scale (by 2013) is still debatable.

During his career as an observer of management, Drucker's prescriptions have been less readily accepted than his insights, such as his devastating critique of the evolution of political organization from nation state to megastate and then beyond to today's "transnationalism, regionalism, and tribalism". In his view, the trio "are rapidly creating a new polity, a new and complex political structure, and one without precedent." The question is how, with only the tools of the nation state and its government to hand, the "performance capacity" of government is to be restored. Drucker comes down decisively against using "the fiscal state" to redistribute income: that, he asserts, merely produces "the pork barrel state", with its "legalized looting" of the commonwealth.

**"That knowledge has become *the* resource, rather than *a* resource is what makes our society 'post-capitalist'. It changes... the structure of society. It creates new social dynamics. It creates new economic dynamics. It creates new politics."** *Post-Capitalist Society*

# Forming the social sector

The state should rather focus on creating the "right climate" for economic well-being. Drucker contrasts this with trying to control the economic "weather", which he disparages. The proper aim of fiscal policy, he says, has to be encouragement of a benevolent climate, by "investment in knowledge and in the human resources, in productive facilities in business, and in infrastructure".

But this in itself will not solve the social problems that so far have been tackled mainly by government. Drucker accuses "the nanny state" of having had "very few results". So he offers an alternative: "...where we have had non-governmental action by autonomous community organizations, we have achieved a great deal. The post-capitalist society and the post-capitalist polity require a new, a social sector — both to satisfy social needs and to restore meaningful citizenship and community."

Drucker admits that "citizenship in and through the social sector", through non-profit organizations, communities, and voluntary work, is no panacea. "But it may be a prerequisite for tackling" the post-capitalist ills. For Drucker "community has to become commitment". The last is a word which also rings out loud and clear when Drucker discusses education: the school "will have to commit itself to results". This is among the "major changes" that (he foresaw in 1989) "are ahead" in schools and education. The knowledge society will demand the changes, "and the new learning theories and learning technologies will trigger them off".

There is no ignoring the aspirational tone. Drucker deeply wants to see a greater society, better attuned to the needs of knowledge — and its managers. "We do not have an economic theory of the productivity of knowledge investment – we may never have one. But... we know, above all, that making knowledge productive is a management responsibility," he states. The manager thus returns to centre stage: government cannot run the knowledge society, and neither can market forces. "It requires systematic, organized application of knowledge to knowledge." Management could hardly ask for a nobler role.

## Ideas into action

- Use new measures, such as the balanced scorecard and activity-based costing.

- Develop rigorous methods for gathering information from outside the company.

- Employ people for their knowledge and manage them accordingly.

- Don't search for the "right model" – design your own organization.

- Concentrate on getting good long-term results while summarizing specific objectives.

- Track the company's performance against a strategic plan and specific objectives.

- Make managing knowledge a prime concern in managing the business.

# Managing innovation

**A**re you an entrepreneur? Are you an innovator? Entrepreneurship and management "are only two different dimensions of the same task" according to Peter Drucker. To be a successful entrepreneur, learn how to manage; to be a successful manager, learn how to innovate.

## Winning by ideas

In the knowledge economy, ideas win. Everybody has ideas all the time, but few exploit them to the full. The key is to build continuous innovation into your work. The greater emphasis you place on generating ideas, Drucker argues, the more they will flow.

Drucker urges you to encourage entrepreneurial thinking inside your unit or organization to achieve success outside. Even more important, you need to be purposefully searching the outside world for entrepreneurial opportunities. Assess your own management of opportunities using the questions and analysis below. Are you:

- Constantly looking outside the business, to the customers and the marketplace?
- Getting all the market information you can from customers and suppliers?
- Creatively using the information that comes back from the outside world?
- Watching out for changes that will signal opportunities (as they always do)?
- Organizing the business to take opportunities when they occur?

**PETER DRUCKER**

### Analysis

If you answered "Yes" to three or more questions, you are performing well, but you must strive to improve in the weak areas you have identified. If you answered "No" to more than three questions you need to take action now – you are wasting vital opportunities.

### Encouraging innovation

If these questions do not seem relevant to you in your current role, remember that, in time, your ability to conceive, sponsor, and execute entrepreneurial initiatives will be decisive. Start practising now.

In today's competitive world, a reputation for enterprising ideas can only benefit your career.

# 1 Innovating for the present

Forget the many myths about entrepreneurship – and never rule yourself out because you do not fit the traditional image of an innovator. Innovation is not about taking risks or predicting the future – focus rather on the opportunities of the present.

## Identifying the future

No-one can predict the future, but you can unlock the secrets of the present, which will be more revealing than any crystal ball. Drucker describes the shape of things to come as "the future that has already happened". To identify that future, ask these questions in sequence:

| Where Are We Now? |
| --- |
| What is the current situation of the business? |
| How is the situation changing? |
| How will the changes affect the business? |
| How will the changes affect its competitors? |
| How can the changes be turned to advantage? |

Understanding the present is relevant even to product innovation. Although people cannot buy something that does not exist, remember Drucker's advice: "Innovate for the present". When Edwin Land invented instant photography, he was not anticipating the desires of generations still unborn. He just thought that his contemporaries, like himself, would want to see their photographs immediately. The test of an innovation is that it creates value. So ask:

- If this product or service were available now, would people want it?
- Is the idea better than, and different from, anything currently available?
- If it were on sale, would people pay for it – and pay at a profitable level?

Do not confuse innovation with novelty. Novelty, says Drucker, "only creates amusement", and will not last into the future.

# 2 Exploiting opportunities

Do not confuse innovations with new products. New processes and methods can be more powerful than new inventions. Use innovative products and processes to win lasting competitive advantage.

## Do things differently

Everything you do as a manager, and every operation you direct, can be improved. Improvements can always be made in small steps, and often in large strides. But equally, your competitors can also improve. To stay ahead, you must keep:

- Challenging every assumption in your own operations – ask: "What can be done differently and better?"
- Analyzing and improving on your competitors – ask: "What are they doing differently and better?"

The entrepreneur is always seeking changes and the opportunities that such changes offer. Find creative ways of using change by:

- Looking outside the competition – are there analogies you can draw with other industries to turn into innovative opportunities?
- Studying your own successful changes – where else can you apply these innovations?

PETER DRUCKER

| **Thinking Creatively** |
|---|
| The Japanese success in world markets was founded less on product innovation than on innovative productivity and marketing. Creative thinking led to simple, but highly powerful, improvements. |

Taiichi Ohno was a production expert at Toyoda (later renamed Toyota), a company making textile machinery. To prevent costly breakdowns, he fitted sensors that were able to detect any irregularities and stop manufacture before the trouble became serious. He then drew an analogy between the machines and the employees. Why not let the employees act like the sensors, allowed to stop and start the production line when faults appeared? This simple innovation became the basis of the production system with which the company and its cars led a worldwide manufacturing revolution.

## Changing the rules

Seek ways of doing things so differently that you change the rules of competition to your advantage. Toyota made its cars more quickly and cheaply. Gillette's first safety razors may not have shaved better than its rivals, but selling cheap razors with expensive blades gave the customer a much lower cost per shave. Learn from these examples: establish economic advantage by being radically different.

Look outside to the customer. Analyze what you are supplying or proposing to supply and break it down feature by feature. Rank each attribute by its value in the customer's eyes. Then rank your major competitors in the same way. Compare the results by asking:

- Where do your competitors excel, and where do you excel, on the attributes most valued by customers?
- What can you do to enhance your strengths and exploit your competitors' weaknesses?

### Selecting opportunities

Such a systematic approach will yield more opportunities than you can easily handle. Bear in mind Drucker's general principles of innovation to sort out the great ideas from the not-so-good:

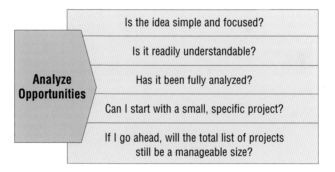

| Analyze Opportunities | Is the idea simple and focused? |
| | Is it readily understandable? |
| | Has it been fully analyzed? |
| | Can I start with a small, specific project? |
| | If I go ahead, will the total list of projects still be a manageable size? |

### Minimizing risk

Drucker does not include taking excessive risks in his warnings, because he equates risk not with unpredictability but with ignorance. The more you know about what you are doing, the less risk you run. You can define risks and seek to limit them, but you are really interested in opportunities. The biggest risk is missing them. Look back on any missed opportunities in your own career. Why did you miss them? Use your past mistakes to learn how to recognize opportunities and embrace change in the future.

**PETER DRUCKER**

### Exploiting the unexpected

At any time things can happen that were neither predicted nor expected. Drucker maintains that unexpected, challenging developments are major sources of opportunities. They provide chances to break the mould. Most people either ignore unexpected successes, failures, or events, or they ignore their significance.

Managers are often expected to do the impossible – make accurate predictions, for example. Every budget and business plan is an exercise in futurology. Drucker insists instead on focusing on what is known and turning that knowledge into future opportunities. Look, for instance, at the sales of one product and ask:

- Why did this unexpected success or failure occur?
- What do those reasons teach me?
- How can I exploit what I have learnt?

### Assessing opportunities

Selecting the right opportunity is crucial. Drucker recommends four different strategies that can turn opportunities into profitable action. Decide which of these strategies can be applied to your opportunity:

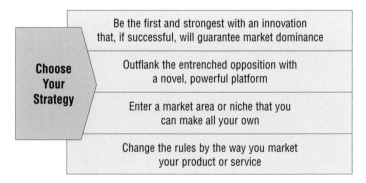

**Choose Your Strategy**

Be the first and strongest with an innovation that, if successful, will guarantee market dominance

Outflank the entrenched opposition with a novel, powerful platform

Enter a market area or niche that you can make all your own

Change the rules by the way you market your product or service

Unless you pursue one of these strategies, or have another, clearly defined and effective strategy of your own, you should not proceed. Your ultimate test is not the amount of entrepreneurial and innovatory zeal you can display, but how successful you are in creating new enterprises and effective advances. As a Japanese sage once taught: "Never let an opportunity pass by, but always think twice before acting".

# 3 Starting new ventures

A new product or service may be launched either from within an established management system or from a brand-new operation. Either way, see autonomy as a precondition of success.

## Acting independently

While independent companies may have no greater entrepreneurial ability, at least they do not have to argue with superiors or put up with interference. They can more readily fulfil their potential.

| The Advantages of Independence |
| --- |
| Analyzing all the available opportunities |
| Selecting the best opportunity |
| Exploiting the chance to create a new, profitable business |

In contrast, the in-company venture enjoys the benefits of the company's greater resources and reputation. But, Drucker warns, established business is also "the main obstacle to entrepreneurship".

## Developing new ventures

Drucker argues that there are five fundamental requirements for the successful management of a new venture:

| The Five Critical Success Factors for New Ventures |
| --- |
| **1** Focusing on the market |
| **2** Planning and re-planning cashflow and capital needs |
| **3** Building stronger management systems than you need now |
| **4** Deciding clearly on your own personal role |
| **5** In an established business, insulating the new venture |

Getting autonomy for a new in-company venture may help it operate more like an independent. Whatever the circumstances, take a professional, managed approach to bring about successful innovation.

# GLOSSARY

**ABANDONMENT:** Dropping unproductive activities after a company looks at its products, services, policies, and distribution channels, and asks itself crucial questions, such as "If we were not doing this already, would we be starting it now?".

**ACTIVITY-BASED COSTING:** A method of obtaining more accurate cost data by allocating overheads and other indirect costs to specific activities required to make products or serve customer segments.

**BALANCED SCORECARD:** Rating performance under headings, of which only some are financial.

**BENCHMARKING:** Examining the operating standards of other companies to improve performance.

**BUSINESS X-RAY:** Determining how much innovation a company requires to stay competitive, in which areas, and within which time frame.

**CORE COMPETENCIES:** The unique abilities that give a particular firm competitive advantage.

**CUSTOMER FOCUS:** Placing a high emphasis on understanding the company's customers and their needs, and making those needs central to decisions about products or services.

**DECENTRALIZATION:** Devolving decision-making from the centre of an organization to give smaller units more responsibility and autonomy.

**ECONOMIC VALUE ADDED (EVA):** Deducting the total financing cost of equity and other capital from a business's recalculated profits to determine its true economic return.

**EMPOWERMENT:** Giving greater responsibility and control to individuals in order to increase employee satisfaction and motivation.

**FEEDBACK ANALYSIS:** An exercise in which expectation is compared with outcome, and steps are taken to improve future performance.

**INCENTIVE COMPENSATION:** Paying for achievement in order to enhance performance.

**KNOWLEDGE WORKER:** "The man or woman who applies to productive work ideas, concepts, and information rather than manual skill or brawn" (*The Age of Discontinuity*).

**MANAGEMENT BY OBJECTIVES:** A technique originated by Drucker to improve individual and group performance, in which managers at every level of an organization have measurable goals that fit the overall goals of the organization.

**POST-CAPITALIST:** Drucker's term for modern society, in which knowledge, rather than capital investment, has become the dominant economic force.

**PRICE-LED COSTING:** When a company starts with what the customer is prepared to pay for the product or service, and then works backwards to calculate what production costs must be targeted.

**PRODUCTIVITY INFORMATION:** Data that relate output to the key resources used, predominantly labour.

**PROFIT CENTRES:** Units within large companies that are responsible for minimizing costs and maximizing revenue for the products or services they provide for the organization.

**RELATIONSHIP RESPONSIBILITY:** The moral responsibility of every manager to communicate reasons and plans to both superiors and subordinates.

**THEORY OF THE BUSINESS:** The "assumptions on which the organization has been built and is being run" (Drucker).

**VALUE CHAIN:** The progress of a product from raw material to sale.

PETER DRUCKER

# BIBLIOGRAPHY

Peter Drucker has written some 30 books in a writing career that spans seven decades. They fall into three broad categories: management studies, socio-economic-political studies, and collections of essays and articles that cover the whole range of his thought. His immense reputation rests on his management books, to which he has continued to add throughout his career.

While deservedly well-respected, Drucker's books on political, economic, and social themes have not had the same acclaim, though their prescience, insight, and originality place them among the leading examples of recent Western thought. Nearly all his books are still in print.

Drucker has also written two novels, *The Temptation to Do Good* (1984, HarperCollins, New York) and *The Last of All Possible Worlds* (1982, HarperCollins, New York). His most read book outside his professional terrain is *Adventures of A Bystander* (1979, Harper & Row, New York), a charming account, ending in the late Seventies, of a life and career of unfailing intellectual distinction and humanity.

## WORKS CITED

Jack Beatty (1997) *The World According to Drucker*, Simon & Schuster, New York.
Peter F. Drucker (1939) *The End of Economic Man*, John Day, New York.
– (1942) *The Future of Industrial Man*, John Day, New York.
– (1945) *Concept of the Corporation*, John Day, New York.
– (1954) *The Practice of Management*, Harper & Row, New York.
– (1969) *The Age of Discontinuity*, Harper & Row, New York.
– (1974) *Management: Tasks, Responsibilities, Practices*, HarperCollins, New York.
– (1984) *Innovation and Entrepreneurship*, HarperCollins, New York.
– (1985) *The Effective Executive*, Harper & Row, New York.
– (1986) *The Frontiers of Management*, Harper & Row, New York.
– (1986) *Managing for Results*, Harper Business, New York.
– (1989) *The New Realities*, HarperCollins, New York.
– (1990) *Managing the Non-Profit Organization*, HarperCollins, New York.
– (1992) *Managing for the Future*, Dutton, New York.
– (1993) *Post Capitalist Society*, Harper & Row, New York.
– (1995) *Managing in a Time of Great Change*, Dutton, New York.
– (1996) *The Pension Fund Revolution*, Transaction Publishers, New Brunswick, NJ.
– (1999) *Management Challenges for the 21st Century*, HarperCollins, New York.
John Micklethwait and Adrian Wooldridge (1996) *The Witch Doctors*, Heinemann, London.
Alfred P. Sloan (1963) *My Years at General Motors*, John Wiley & Sons, New York.

# Index

Page numbers in *italics*
refer to picture captions.

INDEX

# Robert Heller

Robert Heller is himself a prolific author of management books. The first, *The Naked Manager*, published in 1972, established Heller as an iconoclastic, wide-ranging guide to managerial excellence – and incompetence. Heller has drawn on the extensive knowledge of managers and management acquired as the founding editor of *Management Today*, Britain's premier business magazine, which he headed for 25 years. Books such as *The Supermanagers*, *The Decision-makers*, *The Superchiefs* and (most recently), *In Search of European Excellence* have all emphasized how to succeed by using the latest ideas on change, quality, and motivation. In 1990 Heller wrote *Culture Shock*, one of the first books to describe how information technology would revolutionize management and business. Since then, as writer, lecturer, and consultant, Heller has continued to tell managers how to "Ride the Revolution". His books for Dorling Kindersley's Essential Managers series are international bestsellers.